HISTORIC
BATHURST
on the Bay of Chaleur

A. J. McCARTHY

NIMBUS
PUBLISHING

Nimbus Publishing Limited
PO Box 9301, Station A
Halifax, NS B3K 5N5
(902) 455-4286

Design: Joan Sinclair
Printed and bound in Canada

Canadian Cataloguing in Publication Data
McCarthy, A.J.
Historic Bathurst on the Bay of Chaleur
Includes bibliographical references
ISBN 1-55109-303-0

1. Bathurst Region (N.B) -- History -- Pictorial works. 2. Chaleur Bay (N.B.) and Quebec) -- History -- Pictorial works. I. Title
FC2499.B385M26 1999   971.5'12   C99-950213-1
F1044.5.B37M26

Title page: This 1864 Thomas Pye lithograph is of the village of St. Peter. The bridge can be seen in the foreground on the left. Above it is the Presbyterian Church. Near the centre is the high road towards Restigouche, leading straight up from the bridge.

The following sources were consulted for this book:
C.C. Anard, *The Maritime Advocate,* 1951; C.C. Anard, *The Maritime Advocate & Busy East,* 1948; C.C. Kee, *Telephone News,* 1946, "The Story of the Bathurst Exchange"; Richard Edwin Elliott, *White Water and Caulked Boots,* 1978 (booklet); Hardy, Lieut. Campbell, British Army officer, *Rivers of Yesteryear,* 1852; William Hickman, *Sketches on the Nepisiguit,* 1860; Jim Hornby, "The Shantyman's Life" (magazine article), 1976; *The Busy East of Canada,* 1920; Charles Lanman, *Adventures in the Wilds of the United States;* Leonard Lee, *Lower Cove, 150 years later; The Northern Light,* (1951); *The Gloucester Northern Light* (1913–1951); the writings of Cooney, Denys, and Ganong; the Bathurst Heritage Commission; the National Archives, Ottawa; New Brunswick Archives, Fredericton; the New Brunswick Museum, Saint John; George Gilbert, Q.C., booklets; Frank Mersereau, research papers; *Miramichi Advance,* Chatham (1876–1904); *St. Lawrence Advance,* Chatham (1874–1876); *The Commercial,* Chatham (1898–1929); *The Commercial & The World* (1929–1964); *The Gazette,* Chatham (1910–1960); *The Gleaner,* Chatham (1829-1858); *Saint John Daily Sun,* Saint John (1878–1910).

Nimbus Publishing acknowledges financial support for our publishing activities from the Government of Canada through the Book Publishing Industry Development Program (BPIDP), and the Canada Council.

Contents

Introduction iv

Chapter 1
   The Rivers of Bathurst 1

Chapter 2
   The Streets of Bathurst 5

Chapter 3
   The Bridges and Buildings of Bathurst 23
      - Bridges 24
      - Buildings 29
      - Hospitals 72

Chapter 4
   The Industries of Bathurst 75
      - A Grand Celebration 80

Chapter 5
   The Harnessing of the Great Falls 85
      - Light and water come to Bathurst 89
      - Telephones 90

Chapter 6
   Mills, Mining and Lumbering 93
      - Mills 94
      - Mining 102
      - Lumbering 104
      - Life in the Lumber Camps 106

Chapter 7
   Sports of Bathurst 109
      - Horse racing 110
      - Early history of baseball 112
      - Curling in Bathurst dates back to 1883 . . . 114
      - Hockey history in Bathurst 115

Chapter 8
   Transportation in Bathurst 119
      - Railroads 120
      - Old Cars 128
      - Ships 137

Chapter 9
   Fires and Blazes 141

Introduction

Bathurst's early history saw the Mi'kmaq people as its first inhabitants. They made their homes along the shores of the Bay of Chaleur and had their fishing and hunting headquarters at the mouth of the Nepisiguit River. The Mi'kmaq named their headquarters *Winkka Piguwik,* meaning place of troubled waters.

After the arrival of Jacques Cartier in 1534, the Europeans discovered the natural riches of the Bay of Chaleur and they used the area for countless fishing and trading expeditions over the next century. The first missionaries arrived in the bay in 1699 and soon thereafter an influx of pioneers from all parts of Great Britain and France began to arrive.

In addition to the fur trade and fishing, lumbering became an important part of the economy of the Chaleur region. As more and more settlers arrived, farming and the building of wooden ships added to the enterprise of the area.

The earliest settlers called this village "Indian Point"; it was this site that is present-day Bathurst. Indian Point also fell within the Mi'kmaq head-quarters. The area was later named Nepisiguit Village and by the early nineteenth century it was known as St. Peters Village. The village was given the name Bathurst in 1828 in honour of the Earl of Bathurst, then the British government's colonial secretary. The town of Bathurst was incorporated in 1912 and it became a city in 1966.

EARLY SETTLERS   Early settlers came to the Chaleur Region circa 1699.

LOOKING EAST An early 1900s photograph of Bathurst looking east from the Village Hill.

THE NEW BRIDGE Another panoramic view of Bathurst looking east shortly after completion of the new bridge with its familiar arched spans.

THE COVE BRIDGE   A turn-of-the-century photograph, looking north at the Cove Bridge, West Bathurst.

SKATING ON KENT'S POND, c. 1915   In this charming winter scene, people of all ages enjoy the great outdoors, skating on Kent's Pond near the Cove Bridge. The photograph appears to have been taken about 1915. The large homestead in the background is the home of George Kent. The old Superior School can be seen adjacent to Kent's home, partially hidden by trees. The Kent home still stands today while the school has been torn down.

BATHURST POST OFFICE, c. 1900

This early view of Bathurst showing the waterfront was taken around 1900 from the Village Bridge looking South. The old post office, an historic landmark, is the only building, pictured here, still standing.

Chapter 1

The Rivers of Bathurst

PABINEAU FALLS LODGE ON THE NEPISIGUIT

Pabineau Falls Lodge was one of three camps the Bathurst Company had built on the Nepisiguit River to entertain visiting dignitaries and guests. The lodge was located on the south bank of the river at Pabineau Falls and each spring a bridge was erected to span the rapids at the lodge. Two other salmon fishing lodges were also built on the banks of the Nepisiguit at Grand Falls and the Rough Waters Pumphouse. Pabineau Falls Lodge was built in the early 1930s but was destroyed in a fire in the mid-1960s.

Bathurst is built upon two small peninsulas formed by four rivers: the Nepisiguit, the Middle, the Little, and the Tetagouche. The most famous of these is the Nepisiguit which is one of the few rivers in North America that salmon still visit for breeding purposes.

The Mi'kmaq fished the river with spears and traps for centuries before the Europeans arrived. The first salmon caught with an artificial fly was captured by two residents of Bathurst and two English officers in 1845. This marked the beginning of a long history of fly fishing on the Nepisiguit.

In 1850, a fishing expedition to the Great Falls reported the killing of ninety salmon and thirteen grilse in two days despite the fact the group was fishing under great disadvantage, having only one canoe and one gaff between them.

Stories of this great salmon river travelled to Europe and the United States and, by the mid-1850s, sports fishermen were crossing the American border and the Atlantic Ocean to cast their lines in the Nepisiguit salmon pools. Sports fishermen William Hickman and Charles Lanman published extensive papers on the Nepisiguit and each gave a vivid account of the wildlife and flora of the river and its tributaries.

Hickman's narrative provides an enlightening account of sports fishing on the Nepisiguit in 1860. All fishermen crossing the Atlantic were advised to bring their own salmon rods with spare tops; two or three hundred yards of line with winches to match, gaff, and pocket scale. A good flock of feathers for fly making was also necessary, as well as a fireman to ward off bears.

SPORT FISHING AT PABINEAU FALLS ON THE NEPISIGUIT.

The fishermen would make their trip across the Atlantic in ten days by Cunard steamer to Halifax. From there, it took three days by sea or land to the mouth of the Nepisiguit.

While in Bathurst, they stayed in comfort, if not in luxury, at the Wellington Hotel and were outfitted at Smith's General Store.

Before ascending the river, a canoe and two guides were hired to transport the fishermen and their stores to the salmon pools. The guides were expert canoeists and knew every inch of the river. They were also proficient in cooking, repairing rods, tying flies, mending and washing clothes, and making moccasins. For these services, they received a dollar a day.

American sports fisherman and writer Charles Lanman wrote a story about the Nepisiguit River in 1856, published in the *London Illustrated News*. He called the Nepisiguit the most splendid river in the region. And as for salmon fishing with the fly, he stated that, "It had not its superior in the world. It is a marvelous river."

Twenty miles from Bathurst are the Great Falls, impressively beautiful and encased in flint and granite. The total height of these falls is one-hundred-and-forty feet, with deep basins and below them for about a mile, and a number of pools and rapids. The overall impression of this dramatic vista is enhanced by the prevailing roar of the water pounding by, and the blending together of the black water with the white foam.

The cliffs on either side are crowned with dense foliage, kept particularly green by the spray from the falls, and affording a delightful retreat for local birds.

Some seven miles from Bathurst we have what are called the Pabineau Falls—or Cranberry Falls—which consist of a series of chutes and small falls. The rocks which are a gray granite, frequently appear as a massive masonry, so square and regular are they in form.

During the nineteenth century, fishing lodges and camps were built along the river. Hickman describes the daily rituals of one such camp in rich detail:

The camp is raised upon a platform of logs and is situated on the side of a steep hill overlooking the river. The camp itself is divided into three compartments: The first is the sitting room; the next the canoe-men's quarters, who, less refined, combine their sitting-room and bedroom in one; while, beyond that, is the larder, sacred to the cook. The odd little bark hut, with the smoke issuing from its roof, is the curing-house for the salmon....All days in camp are so much alike. With the first light of morning the cook, awakes from his slumber, lights the fire, fetches the water, and rouses the remainder of the party. [Soon] breakfast is smoking on the table consisting of fried pork and biscuit, fried salmon, trout, or oatmeal porridge without milk....Then pipes are lit, rods are carried down the hill to the canoes, and the sportsmen, with their attendants, set out for the pool allotted them, and begin the business of the day. At noon, each returns to camp, relates his adventures, and compares notes of sport with the others; the salmon taken are inspected and weighed, and their size and number duly entered in the journal kept for that purpose. Next follows dinner, consisting of boiler pork or beef, and cold tea.

After dinner the fishermen stretched at lazy length on the fresh-picked spruce boughs, read light literature of the period, others prepare some favourite fly for future conquests; the majority sleep...the canoe-men, seated round its blaze, in turn recount their lumbering adventures, or sing long-ballads. And thus the night wears on until bedtime approaches.

WILLIAM GRAY, GUIDE, C. 1900

In the above circa 1900 photograph, river guide, William Gray, stands in a birch-bark canoe at the mouth of the gorge near the Great Falls on the Nepisiguit River.

Chapter 2

The Streets of Bathurst

ON THE MAIN STREET, C. 1932

Frank Doucet had the first "instant" camera in Bathurst and during the 1930s and '40s he was a familiar sight on the streets of town. With the revolutionary wet-plate camera, he could take a picture and develop the print within twenty minutes. Above, Mr. Doucet poses with his camera on Main Street in this circa 1932 photograph. Leo Cormier, proprietor of Leo's Lunchroom is seen in the background. He was the son of Bathurst's premier photographer, A.C. Cormier.

In 1827 Bathurst's town plot was laid out when Gloucester County was separated from Northumberland. Two years later a town plan was drawn up by Marcus Scully, a New Brunswick engineer.

On December 23 of 1829 a lavish dinner was hosted to celebrate the laying out of the streets of Bathurst. The dinner was held at the London Hotel on Water Street and a full account of the gathering was written up in that week's newspaper: "The dinner was excellent and the wine was good. Perry Dumeresque Esq. officiated in the chair. It was reported the whole group revelled in the uncontrollable enjoyment of all the happiness that emanates from the feast of reason and the flow of soul until prudence suggested the necessity to retreat."

This dinner culminated in the adoption of the "Scully Plan" which is still used today in property searches. In the early years of the town, the streets were not paved and consisted of muddy trails for most of the year. Open ditches lined both sides of the streets and plank sidewalks were put in place in the business districts.

In summer, water was sprinkled on the roadways to keep the dust down and during the winter months the snow drifts were packed down with rollers and horse drawn vehicles rode on top of them. Motorized vehicles were stored for the winter.

In 1934 paving began and in a short while all Bathurst's streets and sidewalks were covered with cement and asphalt.

MAIN STREET, 1940s

Bathurst's Main Street was a busy place in the early part of the 1940s as the above photographs illustrate. Looking east from the Station Bridge one can see vehicles of various makes and models vying for parking spaces and busy shoppers on the sidewalks. None of the businesses featured here remain.

AFTER A WINTER STORM, 1936

The above photograph was taken in the winter of 1936 and shows Bathurst's Main Street after a snowstorm. The large brick building at the left is the W.J. Kent and Co. General Store while the McKenna Bros. Block accommodating the Provincial Bank, Moe Dingott's Clothing Store, and the A.C. Cormier photographic studio stand opposite. Both buildings are gone today as are most of the others in the photo. Walking down the centre of the street is the late Arthur E. Frenette, a well known entrepreneur of the area. Strolling along the sidewalk is Angus Branch. At the time, he was associated with the parent firm of W.J. Kent and Co. Ltd. and was taking the morning mail (from a shared post office box) to Hugh M. Kent who operated a hardware business across the street and slightly down from the big store. The sidewalks were shovelled by hand and huge horse-drawn rollers were used to pack the snow-covered streets, allowing traffic to pass over the top of the drifts. In the spring, when the snow had melted, horse drawn wagons and motorized vehicles sunk to their axles in the rutted and muddy roadways.

SHOPPING ON MAIN STREET, 1920s

The above photographs show how Water Street appeared in the 1920s. Bathurst's Main Street was a busy place back then with retail establishments lining both sides of the street and horse-drawn and gas-powered vehicles travelling the gravel roadway. Busy shoppers can also be seen on the plank sidewalks.

THE NORTH SIDE OF MAIN STREET, 1920s

Bathurst's Main Street was also known, at different times, as Front Street and Water Street. This circa 1920 photograph gives an excellent view of the north side of the street back then.

BLACK STREET IN THE MID-1920S, WITH EDDY'S MILLS IN VIEW

The above photograph of Black Street, taken at the intersection of St. Patrick and Black Streets, shows a very early view of the area. It was probably taken in the mid-1920s, as the streets of Bathurst were paved in 1932. To identify the buildings we called on the expertise of Harold Gammon and Morgan Ruddock, longtime residents of that area of town. To the left of the gravel roadway is Hinton's Bay Chaleur Motors, a rental property, three private homes, Eddy's grist mill, Eddy's planning mill, with its smokestack and chip catcher visible over the roof tops of the homes, and Gus Stout's Coal dealership. In the distance, the Bathurst Company mill yard, smokestacks, and water tower can be seen. Across the street a plank sidewalk runs in front of Rosy Assaff's first store and Eddy's lumber storage building. The white-picket fence surrounds a property now occupied by Hatheway's Ford dealership. What is now Main Street was once called Water Street and extended from the Old Post Office building to the intersection of St. Andrew Street. The section from St. Andrew Street to the mill was known as Black Street.

PARADING ON MAIN STREET, 1930S

A troop of boy scouts led by the Royal Canadian Mounted Police passes through Main Street in this 1930s photograph.

HACHEY'S STORE ON RIVERSIDE DRIVE, c. 1915

This view of Riverside Drive (once called Water Street) looking north towards St. Peter Avenue shows a horse-drawn buggy travelling down a muddy lane; the plank sidewalk leads to the village pump. Visible as well is Hachey's Meat & Fish Store which came into being in 1893 when J.S. Hachey bought the business establishment from Messrs. J. & A. McCullough. The store also dealt in clothing, hardware, groceries, and furniture as well was an outfitter for guides and campers. At the time the photo was taken, about 1915, Mr. Hachey's son, Bennett, had just entered the business as a clerk and he ran the store for several decades thereafter.

WAR'S END ON MAIN STREET, 1918   A parade proceeds down Main Street in this photograph believed to have been taken in 1918, as the event likely commemorates the ending of the Great War. The fire hydrant in the foreground dates the photograph after 1914, the year the water system was installed in the town.

MOTORS VS. HORSES, c. 1930s   This photograph of Main Street was taken in the early 1930s and shows both horse-drawn and motorized vehicles occupying the dirt roadway.

LOOKING WEST FROM KING AVENUE, 1906

QUIETER DAYS ON THE TETAGOUCHE HILL

Now one of Bathurst's busiest thoroughfares, this pastoral scene of the Tetagouche Hill and bridge was photographed early in the century.

LOOKING WEST FROM KING AVENUE, 1906

BOTTOM
LEFT

Probably one of the oldest photographs of Main Street, this picture shows the street, looking west from King Avenue. The 1906 photograph bears no resemblance to today's busy business district. Commercial properties were intermingled with residences of both stately and modest proportions; none of these exist today with exception of the old post office at the far end of the street.

A lady crosses the Village Hill with little concern for traffic in this turn-of-the-century photo. Today this stretch of highway is one of the busiest in the province and the muddy trail shown here has been replaced with four lanes of blacktop.

BUSY DAY ON VILLAGE HILL, c. 1900

TOP RIGHT

The above turn-of-the-century scene shows the Village Hill, looking north. This section of St. Peter Avenue was called King Street back then, and traffic travelled on the left side of the road, as the two horse-driven buggies here are seen doing. At the left, notice the village pump; it was the only source of water for the village residents and was located on the corner of Riverside Drive, then known as Water Street. On the left are Harry Frigault's boarding house, Peter Arseneau's home, Henderson's store, and an unidentified house. Across the Princess Drive intersection is Gus Baldwin's home. On the right side are Dr. Meahan's office, Jack Duffy's Barber Shop, Harry Meahan's home, and Mitch Grant's home. The Holy Family Church is hidden by the trees. Regrettably, all of these buildings are now gone with the exception of Henderson's store.

LOOKING NORTH ON KING AVENUE, PRE-1914

BOTTOM RIGHT

This photograph (bottom right), taken early in the twentieth century, gives a pictorial view of King Avenue, looking north at the St. George Street intersection. The large brick building on the right side is Holdengrabers Store, with Lounsbury's adjacent to it. Both stores burned to the ground in the great Bathurst fire of 1914. At the left is Dr. Densmore's home and the old fire hall with its alarm bell mounted on the roof. The building served as George Allison's blacksmith shop in later years. The mud streets were paved in 1932 and the plank sidewalks replaced with cement, which today have been replaced with bricks. Back then, motor vehicles were a rare sight on Bathurst's streets. Horse-drawn wagons were the most popular mode of transportation. Here, one can be seen in the distance while a sloven can be seen parked at the left. A horse can also be seen standing near the fire hall, possibly "on duty," waiting to be harnessed up if the fire alarm were to sound.

Busy day on Village Hill (above) and looking north on King Avenue (below)

The Streets of Bathurst

KING AVENUE, C. 1920

Here is how one of the city's main thoroughfares looked in about 1920. King Avenue bears little or no resemblance to its present appearance with practically all of the residential and commercial buildings having been replaced. The two exceptions are the Anglican Church and the Porier and Gosslin Store opposite which now houses the RE/Max Offices.

KING AVENUE, SEEN FROM MAIN

A lone stop sign guards the entrance to King Avenue from Main Street. A White Rose service station was the only commercial establishment on the street serving motorists back then, although the building on the opposite corner served as a stagecoach depot in the latter part of the nineteenth century.

GATAIN'S STORE, c. 1910

...and from yet an earlier time the intersection was ever changing—most notable in this circa 1910 photograph is the absence of the standpipe, which was built in 1916. Gatain's store and a stagecoach depot dating back the mid-1800s are seen on either side of the muddy streets bordered by plank sidewalks.

PAVING QUEEN STREET, c. 1934

The above photo shows how street paving was done over sixty years ago. This scene on Queen Street, looking east towards the causeway, was taken around 1934, when the town installed paved streets and sidewalks. Manpower with picks and shovels, along with horse-drawn vehicles, got the job done. More than twenty men and six horses can be seen working on the short stretch of road between Riverside Drive and Thornton Avenue. They were paid about a dollar a day. (You can also see one sidewalk supervisor, leaning on the fence at the left.) From left to right, the buildings are those of Clem Bourdage, and apartment houses owned by the Smith family, and the homes of Azade Landry and Tom Canty.

BATHURST STREET PAVING CREW, c. 1930s

Back in the 1930s, the job of paving the streets of Bathurst was a boon to the men who were out of work during those depression years. This photograph depicts a work crew at East Bathurst pit where they obtained the sand and gravel for the asphalt. The Toronto-based Warren-Bituminous Paving Company was the contractor for the project. Pictured in front of the crusher at the pit site are, from left to right, front: Frank Boucher, Bobby Smith, unidentified, and Sam Frenette. Middle: unidentified, Bili Williamson, Leo Leger, unidentified, Jack Pearce and Tom Doucet. Back: Aloysius Stever, Orvan Bertin, unidentified.

BUSY EVENING ON MAIN STREET, EARLY 1950s

TOP RIGHT

In the early 1950s, Bathurst's Main Street was a mecca for shoppers and residents who wanted some time out on the town. This evening photo shows practically every parking space filled as the locals spend the Saturday evenings downtown shopping and socializing.

LOOKING NORTH ON KING AVENUE, EARLY 1900s

BOTTOM RIGHT

This interesting photo of King Avenue looking north from St. Patrick Street was taken very early in the twentieth century as the streets were not yet paved and plank sidewalks were still in place. The private homes on the west side of the street are all gone, however, the Anglican Church still remains. The large building to the right of the photo was purchased by S. A. McKendy in 1920 and housed a mercantile business for three decades.

BUSY EVENING ON MAIN STREET (ABOVE) AND LOOKING NORTH ON KING AVE (BELOW)

VILLAGE HILL, 1906

This 1906 photograph shows a very different Village Hill than the one we know today. Unobstructed by its present-day buildings, the roadway is much wider and not nearly as steep. Of course, pavement has much improved the muddy rutted street, and there are now cement sidewalks where there used to be plank walkways and ditches. At the left of the photo, looking south, are the Bathurst Company stables and the Mitch Grant home. The small building at the right housed a firehose.

DOUCET FAMILY CELEBRATING CANADA'S DIAMOND JUBILEE, 1927

TOP RIGHT

In 1919, Frank P. Doucet built a store and dwelling place at the corner of King Avenue and St. George Street. His store boasted "large and commodious quarters for his growing business in groceries, confectionery, tobacco, toys and novelties." The building also housed a bowling alley and billiards room. Aside from these ventures Mr. Doucet also ran a bus service. The above photograph was taken in 1927. For Canada's Diamond Jubilee celebration, Mr. Doucet erected a booth near his store with games of "Chance," souvenirs, and refreshments all on offer. He was also a photographer and amateur magician. Mr. and Mrs. Doucet are seen in the booth with their son Vincent. Rudolph Hachey is the gentleman leaning on Mr. Doucet's bus. Doucet's store burned down in 1932 and had, at that time, housed the offices and printing plant of *The Northern Light*.

KING AVENUE, TAKEN FROM FLANNERY'S HILL, C. 1900

BOTTOM RIGHT

King Avenue, now a busy thoroughfare, was just a muddy trail back at the turn of the century when this photograph was taken from Flannery's Hill looking north. The farm buildings and house in the background was the homesteads of Percy and Bert Branch. Notice the cows being brough in for the evening. The house on the left is the home of Martin Doucet.

Canada Day celebrations in downtown Bathurst (Above) and Flannery's
Hill looking north (Below)

HISTORIC HOTEL ON WATER STREET, C. 1920

One of Bathurst's oldest and most pre-eminent buildings was located on Water Street next to Kent's Store. Built around 1830, it originally was the home of some of Bathurst's most prominent citizens. During the 1870s, the Intercolonial Railway was being built and was occupied by Chas Meahan and before him a man named Cowhig. Later, the building was turned into a hotel run under the management of Michael Power. In the subsequent years, the hostelry ran under the banner of Florence, Landry, and Goguen Hotel and under the proprietorship of such well-known local residents as James DeGrace, Jos Landry, Jos Gagnon, A. Goguen, and Edmund Arseneau. The old hotel was the scene of many large gatherings and of much general revelry both in the days when liquor ran free and during prohibition. The hotel shown (above right) in a circa 1920 photograph was torn down in 1932. The house near Kent's Store on the opposite side was the home of Felix Cormier, who was a horse dealer and had his stables situated there.

Chapter 3

The Bridges and Buildings of Bathurst

THE VILLAGE BRIDGE IN 1900.

The Bridges of Bathurst

Surrounded as it is by water, Bathurst is the site of many bridges. The Mi'kmaqs and early settlers crossed these waterways on dugouts and birchbark canoes. Some early attempts to construct suspension and floating bridges at narrower locations upstream were successful to a degree.

In 1829, two major spans were built linking east to west. The bridges were built over the Nepisiguit River and Bathurst Basin. They must have been of poor design as ten years later they were replaced. On April 28, 1838 tenders were offered to construct a new bridge over the basin.

The bridge was to be one-half mile long, twenty-four-feet wide, and built on blocks of sound hemlock or pine logs. The flooring was to be built with three-inch planks. The blocks were to be twenty-four inches by twenty inches at the top, with a thirty-five-inch span from block to block. The spans were to be furnished with three hand rails, spanning the entire length of the bridge. A draw-bridge was to be located at the channel to admit the passage of small vessels. The work was to be completed by July of 1839. The tender document was signed by commissioners Joseph Read, William. Cunard, Chas. Doucett, H.W. Baldwin, and William End. Records show that the bridge was rebuilt again in 1860 by a Bathurst bridge builder, Joseph Morrisson.

By 1840, the East Bathurst bridge (then called the Victoria Bridge) was reconstructed. It spanned the Nepisiguit River and joined the streets of Bathurst to the "Great Road" leading to the Miramichi. On June 2, 1840, as construction continued, a pile driver who was on the bridge along with twelve men were thrown into the river when the dry hemlock used to support them gave way. Another worker, a Mr. James McLellan, was on a scow below and got caught between the falling machine and the craft. He was severely injured and later died. The other twelve men were rescued from the water as they clung to floating timbers.

Only nine years later, the new bridge had deteriorated to the point that one gaping hole in it was so large that a boy fell through it and drowned. Over one hundred feet of the railing was missing, putting in great danger the people and horses who crossed over it.

By 1898, a splendid three-span iron bridge over the mighty Nepisiguit had replaced the old wooden structure. The bridge was again replaced in 1943. The link that presently spans the Nepisiguit was built in 1987. Prior to the construction of a bridge, travellers were ferried across the Nepisiguit River by a scow. Both man and beast were taken across by ferry; Robert Tobin, a well-known Bathurst ferryman, was killed while transporting some oxen over the river. The oxen became agitated at mid-stream, milling about and tipping the scow. Mr. Tobin was thrown from the barge and drowned.

Largely due to poor workmanship and design, bridges leading into Bathurst have been repaired and rebuilt many times in the past century. The old village bridge was replaced in 1938, with a unique half moon steel structure. It stood as a landmark until 1998 when it was replaced with today's four span link.

The Station Bridge, or causeway as it is called today, was built in 1889 by a Shippegan contractor by the name of Arcade Landry. It was washed out by a huge storm in 1940 and stood in a delapidated state until 1956 when it was repaired and resurfaced. Of course, smaller bridges, like the covered bridges that spanned the Little and Middle rivers have been replaced as well as the Cove and Tetagouche Bridges.

STEEL SPANS OF THE EAST BATHURST BRIDGE.

THE EAST BATHURST BRIDGE C. 1896.

NEW BRIDGE CONSTRUC- TION, 1943

The first bridge to span the Nepisiguit River at East Bathurst was built in 1829. Prior to that, the trip across the river was made by ferry boat. The ferry landing was near St. John Street, which was commonly called Ferry Road. The bridge was replaced in 1840 and again in 1898 with an iron-span bridge. In 1943, a wooden bridge that spanned the full width of the river was built. The above photograph shows the new bridge under construction in the summer of 1943. A temporary causeway was built to accommodate traffic during construction.

Storm destroys Village Bridge, 1936

The Village Bridge was damaged by a huge storm in 1936 and was replaced with a new steel span link.

The Station Bridge after the great storm of 1940.

THE STATION BRIDGE C. 1900.

The Buildings of Bathurst

When Bathurst's street plan was laid out in 1829 there were only ten buildings in the town, amongst them a jail, which was a log cabin located on Water Street and a store owned by Joseph Read was also located on Water Street near the Bathurst basin. A Protestant Church stood on Market Street, now Douglas Avenue. There were seven dwelling places, including three lots owned by Joseph Read and one on a lot assigned to the shipbuilder, Joseph Cunard.

A building on a lot at the east end of Water Street, where it intersects with St. Andrew Street, was the home of William Stevens, a businessman who operated a magnesium mine on the Tetagouche River. It survived well into the twentieth century, remaining at the same location until 1990 when it was torn down to make way for a coffee shop. Other registered property owners with dwelling places on their lots were Isabel Levine, Chas. J. Peters Jr. and William Carman.

THE COURT HOUSE, 1900

Bathurst's first court house was built in 1827. It was a two-storey brick building roofed with slate obtained from a quarry on Tetagouche River. The building was allowed to fall into disrepair and was replaced by a fine granite structure in the year 1900. The above photograph shows the court house as it looked shortly after completion. The building, enlarged in 1953, still serves as a court house today.

THE DEGRACE HOTEL, 1930

The DeGrace Hotel was a very popular spot indeed when this picture was taken in the summer of 1930. The hotel opened in 1922 in the former residence of Samuel Napier by Ubald DeGrace and his wife Amanda DeGruchy of Grande-Anse. Mr. Napier, a one-time resident of Bathurst, had moved on to Australia where he became quite well-known for the discovery of the Napier Nugget, the largest gold nugget ever found, a replica of which can still be viewed at the British Museum in London, England. Following his departure, the house was passed on to Thomas Miller, the husband of one of Mr. Napier's daughters. Mr. Miller, a merchant, bought fish from fishing craft owners who tied up at the wharf next to his residence. The building was then owned for a short time by Mr. Archie Chapman and was acquired in 1922 by Mr. DeGrace who, following the addition of a wing to the rear of the building, opened it for business. As one can see from the number of vehicles in the picture, the hotel did very well and a motor coach ferried passengers to and from the two Bathurst train stations, the Intercolonial on Thornton Avenue, and the Caraquet Railway on Bridge Street in East Bathurst. In March 1964 the building was demolished to make way for a modern motel.

BATHURST GRAMMAR SCHOOL BUILDING, 1904

The Bathurst Grammar School was built in 1885 to replace an original structure located on the same St. Andrew Street site and built in 1863. Its predecessor was then relegated to the back of the lot to be used as a woodshed. The new school, measuring fifty-eight feet by forty-five feet, was constructed at a cost to the district of $3,000, and was described at the time by school inspector George Mersereau as a "commodious building filling a long-felt want." It was two-storeys high, had four large classrooms, besides halls and cloakrooms. The teaching staff comprised Principal F.B. Meagher, Helen Meahan, and Carrie M. Walsh with a total of 130 pupils. The grammar school continued to operate for forty-one years until a new school was built on King Avenue. The old wood frame grammar school building was then acquired by the Town of Bathurst to be used as town hall, fire, and police stations. Then in 1959, these venerable civic headquarters were razed to make way for a new town hall. The photo above shows the old school building after it was converted to a town hall and fire station in 1904.

THE ORIGINAL BANK OF MONTREAL PREMISES

The wooden-framed building pictured above was the original premises of the Bank of Montreal in Bathurst. When the bank first established itself here, it operated in quarters rented in the Court House on St. Patrick Street. In 1902, the bank moved to a location at the northern corner of King Avenue and Main Street. In 1919, the Bank of Montreal moved their offices once again, directly across the street to a new sandstone building. Presently, the bank is located at the same location as the original site.

THE BANK OF MONTREAL'S PREMISES IN 1919

TOP RIGHT   The sandstone Bank of Montreal building built in 1919 still stands at the southern corner of Main Street and King Avenue and houses a restaurant.

VIENNEAU'S BARBER SHOP, LIQUOR STORE IN 1920

BOTTOM RIGHT   The above pictured building was constructed in 1918 and still stands today. Back in 1920 when the photograph was taken it was occupied by Mr. S.P. Vienneau, who operated a barber shop and liquor store at the King Avenue location. It is interesting to note that Bathurst had eleven liquor stores before the advent of Prohibition.

BANK OF MONTREAL BUILDING (ABOVE) AND VIENNEAU'S BARBER SHOP (BELOW)

ST. GEORGE STREET OPERA HOUSE EXTERIOR (ABOVE) AND INTERIOR (BELOW)

THE ST.
GEORGE
STREET
OPERA
HOUSE

TOP LEFT

Bathurst's first actual theatre was called the Opera House, a misnomer, perhaps, because this type of high-class musical fare was never offered. Dramatic and musical presentations, mostly by travelling troupes of the vaudeville variety, were the order of the day. The first Opera House was established by Peter J. Leger in 1910. It occupied the second storey of a Main Street building facing Kent's Co. Ltd.. In 1914, fire protection regulations forced its closure and Mr. Leger erected the St. George Street building pictured here shortly after motion pictures arrived on the local scene.

This second Opera House was destroyed by fire in April of 1922. Likewise, the structure of the somewhat similar facade which replaced it was ravaged in the early 1930s. Concurrent with its renovation and reopening a short time later, Mr. Leger introduced "talkies" to Bathurst audiences.

OPERA
HOUSE
INTERIOR
BOTTOM LEFT

This photograph depicts the ornate splendour of the screen and orchestra pit of the first St. George Street Opera House. The theatre orchestra provided background music for the silent movies that played in the Opera House back then.

THE
CAPITAL
THEATRE,
1927

The third generation of the Opera House, later named the Capital Theatre, built immediately after the original George Street Opera House burned, held a gala grand opening on September 22 of 1922. The theatre played to a full house for every performance. The movie shown at the gala was a thirteen-reel epic called *The Four Horsemen of the Apocalypse*. The admission price was seventy-five cents, plus three cents war-tax for the evening show; fifty cents plus two cents war-tax for the matinee, and twenty-five cents plus one cent war-tax for children. The above photograph shows the Opera House decorated for the 1927 Victoria Day celebration.

THE KENT THEATRE

Back in 1952, the Kent Theatre opened, giving Bathurst's movie-goers two theatres to choose from; each one playing double bill matinees daily as well as two performances each evening. The Kent Theatre staged a gala grand opening on January of that year with a presentation of *Here Comes The Groom* starring Bing Crosby and Jane Wyman. For the matinee performance, adults paid thirty-three cents and children fifteen cents, while the evening movie fare was forty-four cents and twenty-seven cents. The theatre operated until 1996 when the final curtain came down.

MOVING PICTURES NEAR THE GLOUCESTER HOTEL, MID-1920S

The above photograph, taken near the Gloucester Hotel in the mid-1920s, shows a power generator mounted on a pickup. John Leger owned the hotel at the time and he was also a pioneer in hydro-power generating. He was the first to construct a power dam at the Tetagouche Falls, at the beginning of the twentieth century. To this day, remnants of his enterprise can still be found there. On hand for that long-ago demonstration were, from left, Dan Frazer, reporter; Art Leger, lecturer; J. Hachey, forest warden; and Roy Hanning, operator. John Leger was a brother of Peter Leger, who owned the Capital Theatre in Bathurst.

During the 1920s, the provincial government produced a documentary film on forest fires and Mr. Leger was commissioned to travel the province to show the film which promoted the value of forestland and encouraged fire safety in wooded areas. Next to the car, one can see a moving picture projector complete with portable generatorthe projector device which is wired to the Gloucester Hotel Building.

THE OLD POST OFFICE, CONSTRUCTED IN 1885

Still standing as majestic as ever at the west end of Main Street is Bathurst's old Post Office and Customs House. Built of sandstone, hauled from Grande-Anse, a distance of some forty miles, and designed from a plan by an architect named Fuller, its style is what is known as Second Empire and was a very popular architectural model near the turn of the century. The building was constructed in 1885; it served as the town's Post Office and Customs House until the early 1960s.

In the early part of the nineteenth century, mail travelled between towns and villages by Stage Coach and Pony Express. "Indian runners" were also used as a courier service. Phil Loosen's grandfather, Theodore DesBresey, was a lawyer in Bathurst in the mid-1800s and he did extensive legal work for a Rexton, New Brunswick shipbuilder. He delivered the legal documents to the company, some eighty miles by an Indian runner who covered the distance in forty hours on foot. The first post office at Bathurst was a pair of Wellington boots—it is not to imply that the postmaster was like the old woman who lived in a shoe, but the post office was located in his private dwelling and the mail was so limited, the postmaster used his old discarded Wellington boots in which to keep the mail. One boot was for incoming letters while the other was for out-going mail.

THE QUEEN HOTEL, LATE 1940S

The Queen Hotel was built at the beginning of the twentieth century by Azade Landry, a prominent businessman and one-time Mayor of Bathurst. In 1920, the property was acquired by Donat Doucet, who also ran a food store and coal business. A very ornate bar, a relic of pre-Prohibition times, was kept intact and served as a conversation piece and as an attraction for visitors. The popular hostelry was located near the CN Railway Station and received weary train travellers from all parts of the country. The building went up in flames in 1953. The above photograph appears to have been taken in the late 1940s.

EARLY BATHURST INN

One of Bathurst's first inns, The White House, was located at the north end of Douglas Avenue, on Main Street. It was built before the end of the nineteenth century and was a popular hostelry until 1921 when it was burned to the ground and never rebuilt.

NEPISIGUIT HOTEL

Lot No. 44 in downtown Bathurst, which Joseph Cunard of Shipbuilding fame owned for four months back in 1841, later became the location for the Nepisiguit Hotel. The hotel, which was built in 1914, by a Mr. Jaillet and carried his name, was later re-named Nepisiguit and subsequently Carleton Hotel. The Carleton was a popular dining and gathering place for many years. It was torn down in 1993 and the lot has since reverted to the state it was in Cunard's day—vacant. 'Nepisiguit' has been spelled a variety of ways over the years, the inscription on the old hotel being one while the most popular and historically accurate.

MCKENNA BROTHERS' BUILDING ON MAIN STREET, C. 1922

RIGHT

The McKenna brothers started a business in Bathurst in 1884 as tailors and clothiers. For many years they were the only firm in their line of business in the community and, in addition, they carried on many trading enterprises and operated a large livery stable. They remained in business until 1930. They were also some of the largest property-holders in the town. The building shown at right is one of the buildings on Main Street that was owned by the McKenna brothers and it was where they operated their clothier business from at one time. It was located on the north side of Water Street, about where a parking lot is located today. Sometime during the late 1920s, the building was consumed into a larger building known as the Pinault block, one also owned by the McKennas. This photo was taken around 1922 when Bathurst's streets were muddy trails and its sidewalks were made of planking. Moe Dingott, a leading Bathurst businessman and philanthropist is standing in the doorway and the other gentleman is one of Bathurst's pioneer physicians, Dr. Duncan.

The McKenna brothers' building on Main Street, c. 1922

THE HOME OF JOSEPH READ, LATER BECOMING THE BRUNSWICK HOTEL

One of the oldest buildings left standing in the downtown area was built by Joseph Read, a prominent businessman in Bathurst's early years. He operated a sawmill at the mouth of the Little River and carried on a business in Bathurst. He arrived from England around 1820 and a town plan from 1828 shows he had a home on the corner of Water and King, as well as a wharf at the north end of King Avenue. The map also shows he had a store on Water Street, about where the Old Post Office stands today. Aside from being a major land-holder, he held many positions of importance. He was collector of customs, deputy treasurer of Bathurst Ports, a Justice of the Peace, and Justice of the Inferior Court of Common Pleas. He was elected to the House of Assembly as a member for Gloucester County in 1846, and re-elected in 1850, 1851 and 1856.

In 1828 there were only seven dwelling places (three of them belonging to Joseph Read), a jail, a church, and a store in Bathurst. One of Mr. Read's houses was located on King Avenue, close to Water Street, but some years later, probably around 1840, he built a new one, a large three-storey dwelling with a Mansard roof, which was a popular architectural design of that era. (The building still stands at the same location on King Avenue.) Mr. Read died on Nov. 19, 1862 and P.J. Burns, the first Mayor of Bathurst, took possession of the property around 1885. The building changed hands a number of times, and in 1925, Frank Fournier acquired it and converted it into a lodging house known as the Brunswick Hotel. The above photo shows the hotel as it looked in 1927.

MOE DINGOTT'S STORE, 1949

When this photo was taken back in 1949, Moe Dingott's store was celebrating twenty-five years in business. The popular men's and ladies' wear store was located in the heart of downtown Bathurst and was one of the most popular establishments around. Moe Dingott also celebrated his fiftieth birthday in 1949 and a gala event was held on May 9 to celebrate both events. Mr. Dingott came to Canada from his native Suczava, Romania and arrived in Bathurst in 1923. In addition to being an enthusiastic supporter of local baseball and hockey teams, he was also a staunch supporter of curling and was a playing member of the Bathurst Curling Club. He was an amateur photographer and his moving pictures of events in Bathurst and the beauties of scenic Gloucester County were masterpieces of photographic art. Just visible in right of the photograph is a parked vintage Pontiac, circa 1937.

WHELAN'S CLOTHING, 1927

In January of 1923, J.P. Whelan's Store was damaged by a fire that also burned the business establishments of Comeau & Co. and Ernest J. Palmer. Again, in November of that same year, his store suffered more damage when a fire broke out in nearby Meahan's Pharmacy. The store and residence of M.J. Kent were also damaged, as well as Dr. W.H. Coffin's office. This photograph, taken in 1927, shows the Whelan clothing store still prospering at a new location about where Frank's Furs is located today. The building shown at the left is Fatty Kent's Bakery.

STEDMAN'S STORE

TOP RIGHT

The Stedman 5¢ to $1.00 Store in Bathurst was originally located in the Main Street store of J.P. Whelan. The retail business had so advanced by 1934 that it warranted the establishment in Bathurst of a branch of the large chain of Stedman stores and a fine new building was erected that year. The original building still stands today on Main Street, but has been much altered with apartments on the second level. Stedman's department store was a popular shopping centre for Bathurst residents for many years. In the early 1970s, the store moved to a new, larger location, also on Main Street, opposite the Eddy Building. However, it closed shortly thereafter, due to a lack of business. The store sold clothing, appliances, and toys, and had a lunch counter.

MAIN STREET INTERSECTION, 1930S-40S

BOTTOM RIGHT

The intersections at Main Street, St. Peter Avenue, and Douglas Avenue have seen many changes over the years. Even the street names have changed. St. Peter Avenue was once known as Restigouche Road and Main Street was originally called Water Street. The photograph at bottom right shows how the corner looked back in the late 1930s and early '40s. The area directly opposite the Old Post Office has been occupied by one service station or another since 1919 when Alfred Veniot built a garage there. In addition to servicing the needs of the motoring public, he also sold Pontiac and LaSalle automobiles in the 1930s and early 40s. Mr. Veniot gave up his automobile franchise in the 1940s and rented his showroom space to the government to use as a liquor store. A Pontiac Sedan of that era can be seen in the photo. A bus belonging to the much relied-upon (and still operating) Bathurst, Shippagan, and Tracadie Gloucester Motor Coach Line can also be seen in the photo.

STEDMAN'S STORE (ABOVE) AND MAIN STREET INTERSECTION (BELOW)

THE FAMOUS GATAIN'S, CORNER OF MURRAY AND ST. GEORGE

For a substantial portion of the twentieth century, Gatain's at the corner of Murray Avenue and St. George Street as it merges into lower Main, was one of the town's busiest centres of activity. Dating back to 1910, the main building housed a grocery, fruit, and confectionery store. Frank Gatain, owner and manager, specialized in fancy goods unavailable at the time anywhere else in that area.
A popular item in the store was Slipp and Flewwelling sausages imported every weekend from Saint John. Mr. Gatain also introduced a soda fountain and ice cream parlor to Bathurst, and later, one of Bathurst's first badminton courts. For many years prior to that, two tennis courts were located on the same property, also owned by Gatain's. Tournaments, involving the other North Shore towns, were always social and sporting highlights during the summer months. But perhaps the most popular attraction was a large dance hall adjoining the store which which welcomed visitors from around the province as well as Bathurst residents on Saturday nights, or other special occasions. For the most part, local orchestras provided the music and crowds danced late into the night at the town's principal cabaret.
In the early 1940s, Frank Gatain retired due to poor health. The property was sold, moved back from the street, and converted into an apartment complex which has since disappeared from the landscape.

KENT LODGE, HOTEL TO THE RICH AND FAMOUS

On the Dominion Day holiday weekend of 1936 Kent Lodge opened. Over two hundred invited guests attended a formal ball and it was said to be the most spirited and elegant function ever presented on the North Shore. Gloucester Branch No. 18 sponsored the opening ball to raise funds for the soldiers's monument, or cenotaph, that now adorns the Court House grounds on St. Patrick Street. Kent Lodge flourished for over two decades, principally catering to Upper Canadian guests who included celebrities like Prime Minister Louis St. Laurent and members of his family; Hon. C.D. Howe, the federal cabinet minister; Gerald (Chubby) Powers, another well-known government figure; Lord Beaverbrook, Sir James Dunn, the Dawson family of Scotland, of Scotch whisky fame; CCF Leader M.J. Coldwell; Col. Billy Bishop, the First World War air ace; Conservative Party Leader, R.J. Manion; Hon. J.L. Ralston, Minister of National Defence during the Second World War; Lionel Conacher, the hockey great; Col. John Price, of Price Bros., who commanded the Royal Rifles of Canada during the Hong Kong siege and who afterwards offered the survivors jobs in his company's paper mills; Judge Andre Taschereau, a Quebec Superior Court judge.

These prominent personalities, along with other guests, were enticed to the Chaleur and Youghall Beaches by their clean sands and warm waters and the splendid facilities offered by the hotel owners which made Kent Lodge a welcome haven from the stifling heat of the cities. It was ironic that the Legion which had so ceremoniously opened the lodge, permanently (and inadvertently) closed the hostelry twenty-two years later; following a convention of the war veterans' group, Kent Lodge was completely destroyed by fire during the Labour Day weekend of 1958.

W.J. KENT & COMPANY BUILDING

In 1884, when W.J. Kent established a retail mercantile in Bathurst, he operated out of a small wooden building on Water Street. In 1902 a new two-storey brick building was constructed to accommodate the steadily increasing patronage. By 1914 business had grown to such an extent that Mr. Kent had to enlarge his store to twice its original size. After a fire gutted the store in 1915, a third storey was added making the department store one of the largest in Eastern Canada. W.J. Kent & Company Limited was the leading mercantile in Bathurst for many years until its demolition in 1990.

OLD IRVING STATION ON MAIN STREET, c. 1940

TOP RIGHT

A landmark on Main Street for many years was the old Irving service station located at the King Avenue intersection. The station was built in 1934 and served the motoring public until 1991 when it was torn down. This circa 1940 photograph shows the Caraquet and Grande-Anse motorcoach taking on fuel. The Brunswick Hotel looms in the background.

MI'KMAQ LODGE LUXURY HOTEL FOR SUMMER GUESTS

BOTTOM RIGHT

The Mi'kmaq Lodge was the first luxury hotel built exclusively for summer use. George L. Kelly welcomed the first guests to his new lodge in the spring of 1932, among them the family of Thodore Morgan of Henry Morgan and Co. of Montreal. The inn was located at Youghall only a five-minute walk from the beach. The splendidly appointed summer resort received visitors from all parts of the continent during the two years that it operated. On June 7, 1934 it burned to the ground.

OLD IRVING STATION ON MAIN (ABOVE) AND MI'KMAQ LODGE (BELOW)

THE ROBERTSON HOUSE HOTEL, EARLY 1900S

The Robertson House was one of the premier Bathurst hotels of its era. Built and owned originally by James Carey, who later immigrated to Boston, the forty-room hotel was then acquired by the Robertson family. The Robertson House was located on the present site of the Royal Bank and it, along with its gardens and outbuildings, including stables and sample rooms occupied about half that entire block. A very ornate bar-room occupied the central part of the main floor of the hotel and for hours at a time this remained unstaffed. The honour system, it seems, prevailed among imbibers in those days, and customers poured their favorite brew or brand, enjoyed the drink, and then recorded their purchases on a blackboard installed on the premises. The Robertson House faced Main Street but was set back from the road and the entrance and exit to and from the property was via a circular driveway. Across the street, a stairway descended to the river bank, where rolling grass and trees formed a beautiful bower for hotel guests during their leisure hours. A substantial wharf jutted out into Bathurst Harbour and moored to it were a dozen or so small boats placed there for the convenience of the hotel's clientele. The hotel was built before the end of the nineteenth century and it was destroyed by a fire in 1916 and never replaced.

F.T. FRENETTE'S GENERAL STORE ON KING AVENUE

Back before the days of large chain stores and shopping malls, people did their retail business at the local general store. From the 1920s to the 1940s, F.T. Frenette's General Store on King Avenue was one such enterprise. It was a huge, wooden two-storey structure with the store located on the main floor and the family quarters above. F.T. Frenette's carried a large and varied stock of wares: hardware, clothing, household utensils, groceries, feed and just about everything else farmers and city folks might need. A large shed at the rear was filled with bulk animal feed, hay, and farm implements. A delivery boy was readily available with horse and buggy to convey orders to people's homes. The business was acquired by a local co-op in 1940 and closed shortly thereafter. The building was razed and the lot remained vacant until 1965 when the present Northern Light building was constructed there.

DOUGLAS AVENUE BUILDING, BUILT c. 1870

One of the oldest buildings still remaining in Bathurst's downtown district sits at the north end of Douglas Avenue. Built around 1870, it once housed a telegraph office, provincial police station, and restaurant. In 1885, Mr. William R. Johnson, a telegrapher for the Canadian National Railway bought the building from a Mary Proctor and Mrs. Johnson ran a yard goods store there.

DUFFY'S BARBER SHOP AT THE END OF MAIN STREET

TOP RIGHT

Duffy's Barber Shop stood at the end of Main Street near the causeway for over one hundred years before it was moved in 1970. The old building had many occupants over the years; the first of memory being a Miss Libby Sinclair who operated a confectionery store there. A succession of tenants followed and finally the premises came into the possession of John Duffy, Sr. who operated a barber shop there for many years. Finally the property was sold to Irving Oil and the building was moved.

HOME AND STUDIO OF PHOTOGRAPHER HENDERSON, VILLAGE HILL

BOTTOM RIGHT

The home and photographic studio of one of Bathurst's earliest photographers was located at the foot of the Village Hill. Mr. Henderson photographed early scenes of Bathurst's streets, homes, and businesses hundreds of which still exist today in private collections and at the New Brunswick archives. There are also many of his photographs within the pages of this book. The photograph at bottom right, taken in the 1930s, is typical of the type of photograph he produced in his studio.

DUFFY'S BARBER SHOP (ABOVE) AND PHOTOGRAPHER'S HOME AND STUDIO (BELOW)

LOUNSBURY STORE, c. 1935 A section of King Avenue circa 1935 shows the Lounsbury Store as it looked back then. It was one of many buildings the company occupied in the town since its conception in 1897. The adjoining building is Holdengrabers Store.

HOME OF ROYAL BANK IN BATHURST, MID-1930S

TOP RIGHT When the Royal Bank came to Bathurst, they set up shop in a building on Main Street that also housed Meahan's Clothing Store. The above photo shows it as it was in the mid-1930s. The building was torn down in 1963.

PINAULT'S HOME AND BUSINESS, ON ST. PATRICK STREET

BOTTOM RIGHT Early in the twentieth century, St. Patrick Street was a busy mercantile center in Bathurst. The two buildings pictured above were located at the lower end of the street and were the business establishment and home of Fred Pinault. Mr. Pinault operated a clothing store during the 1930s.

Home of Royal Bank (above) and Pinault's home and business (below)

The Bridges and Buildings of Bathurst

MAIN STREET BUSINESS CENTRE, 1933

When this photograph was taken back in August of 1933, there were more businesses on Main Street than there are today. There have been many other changes, including the name of the street which was called Water Street at the time of this photo. The large building in the centre of the photograph which housed Bathurst's first theatre and other business establishments, was enlarged and renovated many times, even before 1933. It was later expanded to cover an adjoining lot and was variously known over the years as the Pinault, Sand, and Dalfen block . It housed department stores on the main floor and apartments on the upper levels. Today, there is a parking lot where the building once stood. The building to the right is that of Melanson's grocery store and the Provincial Bank, originally owned by the McKenna brothers, who operated a men's clothing and tailoring establishment. The building shown at the left is one of the few on the street that still stands. It has been renovated, remodelled, and enlarged and today it forms the nucleus of the Sportsman's Tavern where a gruesome double murder took place in 1991. Over the years, the little building has had a litany of owners and tenants including Alex Ward Veterinary supplies, a barber shop, Larry Aubie's taxi stand, Norman Gray's restaurant, Max Starr's restaurant, and Brub Schryer's restaurant.

PROVINCIAL BANK, c. 1930

The original McKenna brothers building was built before the turn of the century and housed numerous businesses for the many years it stood on Main Street. At the time this photograph was taken (circa 1930), the Provincial Bank occupied part of the building while Leo Melanson's grocery store did business next door. The photographic studio of A.C. Cormier was on the second floor. The building was demolished in 1972.

PERLEY DUNN'S MEAT MARKET, c. 1940

The section of King Avenue where the Post Office now resides was once a busy retail district as the above circa 1940 photograph shows. The building at the right is Perley Dunn's meat market. Mr. Dunn was an avid hockey promoter and ran the market from the 1920s to late 1940s. In the adjacent building, S.A. McKendy ran a grocery store and in the same era Frances Lorden had a stationery store there. Both buildings were torn down in 1958 to make way for the post office building.

HOTEL GLOUCESTER

One of Bathurst's finest hotels for many years was the Hotel Gloucester. Built by industrialist P.J. Leger in 1922, it was one of the most modernly equipped in the province. All forty-eight guest rooms had hot and cold running water and eight of them had private baths. The dining room had an area of 736 square feet. The basement featured a pool room, barber shop, and a large sample room for travelling salesmen. It also had a large root cellar to keep fruits and vegetables fresh. Commercial travellers also had access to a well-appointed writing room while female guests were equally as well looked after in a large sitting room opening off the rotunda. The building still stands today on the corner of Main Street and Douglas Avenue.

BUILDINGS AND BUSINESSES OWNED BY A.T. HINTON

GENERAL STORE, TOP RIGHT

EQUIPMENT AND SUPPLY STORE, BOTTOM RIGHT

Hinton's General Store was established by Mr. A.T. Hinton in 1883 and was closely associated with the early history and development of Bathurst. The building shown at top right was built in 1912. It carried an exceptionally large stock of mercantile goods including clothing, groceries, furniture, hardware, meat, fish, and feed. The business prospered until the early 1950s when the property was sold to become the site of Hatheway Motors. Adjacent to the general store was another large building that dealt in farm machinery, gasoline engines, horse-drawn buggies, and harnesses. Mr. Hinton later took on the Ford automobile franchise when the industry was in its infancy. That part of the business which was later re-named Bay Chaleur Motors burned to the ground in 1942. In the circa 1895 photo (bottom right), Mr. Hinton is shown standing in front of his business establishment surrounded by his wares.

BUILDINGS AND BUSINESSES OWNED BY A.T. HINTON

BURNS AND MELANSON WHOLESALE BUILDING, 1927

The above photograph, taken in 1927, shows the Burns and Melanson Wholesale company building, decked out to celebrate Victoria Day that year. The business suffered major fire damage on Feb. 25, 1924, when the building was gutted, and much of the stock of groceries and feed in a warehouse was also damaged. The business establishment would have been a total loss had it not been for the swift thinking of Officers O'Brien and Gammon. They were returning from a liquor raid on an illegal still, when they noticed flames coming from the building and quickly summoned the fire department. The business was later known as Eastern Hay and Feed. In recent years, it served as the home and office of Dr. Leger, a dentist.

LANDRY'S JEWELLERY STORE, 1920

RIGHT

F.O. Landry's Jewellery store and optical parlor opened its doors to the public in 1900 and was considered one of the finest stores of its kind for the era. In addition to a full stock of jewellery, watches, and gramaphones, the business boasted watchmaking, lens cutting, and engraving facettes right on the premises. The above photo was taken in 1920. Mr. Landry remained in the jewellery and optical business until the early 1930s operating out of this Main Street building. The building was destroyed by a fire on December 21, 1945. It housed the Radio Cafe, operated by John Joe Tong at that time. Mr. W.H. Heath, a forty-year veteran of the Waltham Watch factory did the necessary watchmaking and repairs while A.J. Breault did the lens grinding and frilling.

LANDRY'S JEWELLERY STORE, 1927

"THE 5 AND 10 CENT STORE, 1927

The building in the above photo still stands today and houses Cormier's Canteen. Back in 1927, when the photograph was taken, it served as a variety store known as the '5 cent, 10 cent, 15 cent and 25 cent Store.' It was operated by the Landry sisters, Corinne and Lea, who lived in the house next door, shown partly hidden in the trees. That building is also still there today, on the corner of King Avenue and St. Patrick Street. During their tenure the owners were affectionately referred to as "The million dollar ladies with the five and ten cent store."

WILSON'S EMPORIUM ON KING AVENUE, 1938

TOP RIGHT

When this photo was taken in 1938, Wilson's cut-rate store on King Avenue was celebrating its third year in business. The emporium handled a complete line of ladies', men's, and children's ready-to-wear items, including boots and shoes. The establishment was one of the largest and most modern on King Avenue at that time. The business was owned by the Wilson family and managed by Miss Cecilia Wilson. The building housed Holdengraber's department store previous to its occupation by the Wilsons.

THE REBUILT HOLDENGRABERS STORE, C. 1915

BOTTOM RIGHT

Holdengrabers, a reputable clothing and dry goods store, was established in Bathurst in 1897. In the beginning, the business was housed in a large brick building at the corner of King Avenue and St. George Street, opposite the Big Deal, a grocery store. Holdengrabers burned in the great fire of 1914, and the Holdengraber family rebuilt the store, which is the one pictured above. It thrived until the mid-1930s, when Simon Holdengraber and his family moved to the United States.

WILSON'S EMPORIUM IN 1938 (ABOVE) AND THE REBUILT HOLDENGRABER'S (BELOW)

Fenwick Bros. meat market

About 1870, A.J. Fenwick began a meat and provisions business in Bathurst. By 1898 the business had grown and A.J.'s sons, W.G. and Oscar, were successfully operating the merchantry in quarters in the Boss Block (a large building located on Main Street, opposite the Nicolas Denys monument). By 1916 they constructed their own building. It was 50 feet by 60 feet, well constructed and served the wholesale and retail meat needs of the citizens of Bathurst until the mid-1940s. The meat market of Fenwick Bros, was located at the corner of Murray, Main and St. George Street and still stands today. The brothers sold all types of meat: beef, pork, mutton, and corned beef. The specialized in the making of sausages and their Hobart Sausage mill turned out two hundred pounds an hour and usually worked steady to supply the demand. In the above photo W.G. and Oscar can be seen in the doorway of the emporium. A horse-driven delivery vehicle stands ready to unload an additional supply of fresh meat to customers while carcasses of freshly slaughtered animals hang in the window.

WISEMAN BROTHERS ENTERPRISES, ON BRIDGE STREET

Back in 1920, when the above photograph was taken, brothers R.H. and George S. Wiseman were operating successful business enterprises in East Bathurst. Although housed in the same building, they did not form a partnership. Working in close cooperation, each brother handled his own business. George S. established a successful meat and fish business in 1916 and his endeavor was housed in the front of the store. R.H. served in the First World War, seeing action in such famous battles as Vimy, Amiens, Arras, Cambrai, as well as being with the first group of Canadians that broke through the Hendinburg line. Upon his return home in 1919 he set up shop at the rear of the store, selling groceries, dry goods and feed. The two-storey building measuring twenty-five by ninety feet was located on Bridge Street, opposite Maurice's Convenience Store.

MELANSON'S MERCANTILE, 1920

The mercantile enterprise of H.A. Melanson was founded in 1880 by Samuel Melanson. In 1915, the business came under the ownership of his son, H.A. Melanson, a former travelling salesman who had been representing the Montreal firm of Hodson Sumner & Co. in the Maritime provinces. The store was located at the west end of the Village Bridge and was stocked with a complete line of dry goods, boots and shoes, ready-to-wear clothing, groceries, flour, and feed. This photograph was taken in 1920 when the general merchant was doing a brisk business, employing five clerks and serving patrons from not only West Bathurst and the town, but also from the surrounding countryside.

BOYLE'S LUNCH

TOP RIGHT

Back in 1948, Boyle's Lunch, an eating establishment, offering light lunches, refreshments, and a confectionery was opened. The proprietor of the restaurant was Mrs. James F. Boyle and she was assisted by her two sons and three daughters in operating the business. The building was located on a lot directly opposite to the old Capital Theatre. In later years, it served as an SMT bus stop, a Dixie Lee and a beauty parlor. It was removed in the early 1980s to make way for a parking lot.

DESROCHE HABERDASHERY, 1920

BOTTOM RIGHT

Mr. L.L. DesRoche was one of Bathurst's leading haberdashers early in this century. He opened his store in 1908 and his proud boast was that he was "able to clothe a man from head to foot." In addition to running his men's wear store, Mr. DesRoche also devoted much of his time to civic, patriotic, and philanthropic endeavors. He was a town alderman for three years, Captain of a Victory Loan drive during the Great War, and an active member of the Board of Trade, and a staunch supporter of the Red Cross Society. He was a man of good business sense and was a large property holder. The clothier was located on Water Street and the above photograph, taken in 1920, shows Mr. DesRoche and a clerk standing in the doorway of the establishment.

BOYLE'S LUNCH (ABOVE) AND DESROCHE HABERDASHERY (BELOW)

**LEGER'S
HOTELS**

John P. Leger engaged
himself in the hotel
business shortly after he
arrived in Bathurst in
1898 and soon became
one of the town's leading
businessmen. His first
endeavour is shown (top)
in a 1912 photograph
burned down in 1915.
His second attempt
(right) also burned down
and was again replaced
by the building shown
below. All three Leger
Hotels were at the west
end of Queen Street
near the Intercolonial
Railway line and were
among the best-known
hostelries in New
Brunswick at the time.

KENNAH BROS. GARAGE ON WATER STREET

Kennah Bros. Garage began in 1919 and it was located on Water Street (opposite the Royal Bank). The brothers, Jack and Herb, operated in a building originally built in 1900 by George and John Robinson as a warehouse for their lumber operations in Burnsville. By the late 1920s, when this photograph was taken, the garage had become one of the leading establishments for automobile repairs and machine work in the area. The business was also agent for Star and Durant automobiles and a popular meeting place for the community's leaders and local sages. It was there that the topics of the day—sports, politics, and "what-have-you"—were discussed. In the mid-1930s an addition was built on the existing garage and the business served the motoring public until 1968.

VENIOT'S PHARMACY

Veniot's Pharmacy came into being in 1915 and for the first four years operated in quarters located in the Old Opera House on Water Street and was known as the McCarthy-Veniot Pharmacy. In 1919, Dr. C.J. Veniot erected a splendid new building on King Avenue and the company did business there until 1987.

When it opened, the Rexall drug store was hailed as one of the most modern business establishments in Eastern Canada. Special reference was given to a "a big cash register which operated by electricity with provisions for nine different departments, and five cash drawers. This wonderful machine keeps amazing records which tell at a glance the sales records of the day." Another progressive feature was 'spot cash trading.' Every item in the store is bought for cash from the wholesaler and sold for cash to the customer. No books are kept for charge or credits.

PICOT'S GARAGE ON ST. PETER AVENUE

TOP RIGHT

St. Peter Avenue has seen many changes since this photograph was taken in 1940. Shown above is Philip Picot's garage and homestead which was located on the south side of the street where UAP Auto is located today. Mr. Picot served the motoring public with Texaco Sky Chief and Red Indian gasoline and oil, as well as Firestone Tires and auto repairs. In 1950, he sold and serviced Vanguard and Morris automobiles. He also had an automobile scrap yard at the rear of his garage. The selection of vehicles, a Chevy truck, a Ford Sedan, and a Harley Davidson motorcycle of that era add a nice touch to a most interesting photograph.

THE DEPOT HOTEL

BOTTOM RIGHT

At the turn of the twentieth century, Azade Landry was one of the areas leading hoteliers with hotels in Campbellton, Moncton, and Bathurst. Mr. Landry built two inns near the CN railway station in West Bathurst. He erected the Queen Hotel around the turn of the century and the Depot Hotel (shown above) about 1915. The old hotel changed hands many times over the years and was once owned by a Doctor Gregory Theriault. He was a faith healer and practiced at an office in the hotel. He also used the inn as a retreat where the faithful could rent a room and receive treatment to rejuvinate the body and soul. The building, although much changed, remains to this day and serves as an apartment house.

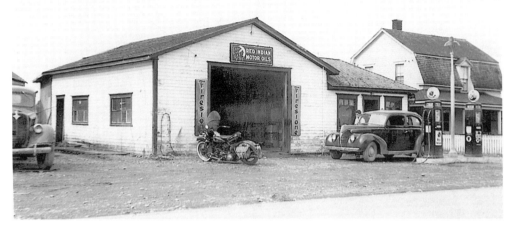

PICOT'S GARAGE (ABOVE) AND THE DEPOT HOTEL (BELOW)

Hospitals

Our Lady of Lourdes of the Lady Dunn Institution was first opened on May 4, 1931. The Sanatorium for the care of tuberculosis patients was located at the Somerset Vale, a one thousand-acre farm which was donated to the Religious Hospitallers of St. Joseph by famous Bathurst-born philanthropist, Sir James Dunn (Lord Beaverbrook).

VALLEE LOURDES, 1933

The picturesque vale where the Religious Hospitallers built their first hospital became known as Vallee Lourdes. The nucleus of the Sanitorium was originally the manor house of Hugh Munro and is believed to have been built shortly after the turn of the nineteenth century. In the above photograph, the hospital is seen shortly before it burned down on Christmas Eve of 1933. The little house on the right served as servants quarters for the wealthy owners of the estate over the years: Hugh Munro, Francis Ferguson, Carr Harris, and during the 1920s Sir James Dunn used it as a summer home. The building along with the barns of the model farm were torn down in the 1970s.

THE DUNN HOSPITAL

Bathurst's first hospital, the Seaman Hospital, was located on Riverside Drive. It was an outpost for first aid during the early days of shipbuilding. It also served the people of the village when the need arose; the hospital was equipped with twelve beds. The Dunn Hospital (above) was established in 1911 from an original gift of $10,000 from Sir James Dunn. With this sum, the hospital's founders purchased the home of Dr. Gideon Duncan which became the Seaman Hospital. After a fire destroyed the original structure in 1917, the new building was enlarged to accommodate thirty-five patients. Overlooking Bathurst Basin, the site, now known as St. Luke Court, was also occupied by St. Luke's Presbyterian Church and adjoining cemetery. The Dunn Hospital, which finally reached sixty-bed capacity, operated in conjunction with Gloucester County's first school of nursing, which was noted far and wide for its excellent training program. Badly damaged by fire in January, 1951, the Dunn Hospital was razed and never replaced.

DR. GIDEON DUNCAN'S HOME

THE GLOUCESTER HOSPITAL, 1927

This 1927 picture of the Gloucester Hospital shows it three years after its opening. The hospital, an endeavour of Bathurst physician, Dr. W.H. Coffyn, had a capacity of sixteen beds with the most up-to-date medical equipment. The hospital occupied the entire second floor of a building on King Avenue then owned by the George Eddy Co. On the north side was the Gray Building while on the south side was the P.S. Andrews residence. The ground floor of the building as occupied by the King Street Pharmacy, Miss Coffyn's Refreshment Parlour, A.I. Tower Ltd., National Shoe Store and Dr. Coffyn's Office. It was Sunday night, Dec. 15, 1940, one of the coldest nights of the year, that tragedy struck. Fire, which according to some reports, began in the furnace room then spread quickly through the hospital which at the time had a total of ten patients including two babies. It was due to the heroic efforts of the nurses that more lives were not lost. Neighbors, members of the 2nd North Shore Regiment and of the Bathurst fire department tried in vain to reach patients trapped in the inferno. A young woman with her child, an elderly resident of Petit-Rocher, and a young girl perished in the fire.

Chapter 4

The Industries of Bathurst

THE PULP MILL, EARLY 1900S

A view of the Bathurst Pulp Mill taken from the East Bathurst
Bridge early in the century.

Nicolas Denys and Jean Jacques Enaud are the first recorded Europeans to settle on the shores of the Bay of Chaleur. Denys, from Tours, France, established a fort at Father's Point (Gowan Brae) near Bathurst in 1635. Remnants of this old brick fort were still standing well into the twentieth century. Enaud was from Basque, France and he put down roots at Alston Point near Bathurst in 1638. He constructed a fortress there and had a Grist Mill at Getty Brook. He also carried out an extensive fur trade with the Indians.

When James Sutherland arrived in 1789 from England he also built his home and fortress at Alston Point. He constructed a brig there and sailed it back to England in a record sixteen days. About 1760, Commodore Walker, a Scotsman, established an extensive trading establishment at Alston Point as well as dwellings at Youghall and on the Nepisiguit River. He also established a salmon fishery on the Nepisiguit below Rough Waters. After Walker left a Dominique Doucet occupied the same lands and operated two wind powered grist mills at St. Peters Village.

The Scottish Hugh Munro came in 1780 and settled in St. Peters Village. He carried on a trading and mercantile business and was collector of customs. He also engaged himself in the timber shipping business. He had mills on Little and Middle Rivers.

Another Scotsman, John Ferguson settled in the village of St. Peters in 1834 and established a business under the name of Ferguson-Rankin & Co. The steam mill was destroyed by fire shortly after being built and another was put up. The new mill also went up in flames on March 31, 1908.

The Ferguson farm was located on the present site of Gowan Brae. Around 1820, Joseph Cunard established a ship building business in Bathurst. It was located on Water Street. At the same time that Cunard was building ships here Joseph Reid was well established in the timber business. He had mills on the Little and Middle Rivers. He was elected to the House of Assembly in 1846.

In 1846 a gentleman by the name of J.C. Ord, who owned a large estate in England, took an interest in the Chaleur region. He made an application to purchase 40,000 acres of land in the county of Gloucester, near Bathurst. His proposal was accepted and he arrived in the Bay of Chaleur, on a steamer on August 19th of that year to take possession of his holdings.

Mr. Ord was impressed with the fertility of the soil and the beauty of the countryside which also possessed many advantages with respect to mining and fishing. He also pledged he would form a mining company and start boring for coal which he believed was in abundance in the region.

Within a few short years grist and lumber mills were being built on almost every river and stream around Bathurst. In 1885, O.F. Stacy built a mill at the mouth of Carter's Brook. His business flourished for about twenty years. In 1909 it was sold to the Bathurst Lumber Company together with a farm in connection therewith.

The Gloucester Lumber and Trading Company was formed in 1903 and controlled two-hundred-and-twenty-five square miles of forestland. The company controlled mills in Bathurst, Burnsville and Petit Rocher.

The Ferguson-Rankin mill was acquired by the Bathurst Lumber Company in 1905 and in 1912 the company purchased the mills and farm of the Adams Burns Company. The Bathurst Lumber Company was the founding company of Bathurst Power and Paper which was built on the site of the Cunard farm and began making pulp in 1915.

Other mills operating in Bathurst were the George Eddy Company which operated a wood manufacturing plant and Grist mill on lower Main Street and MacIntosh Bros. wood-working factory located at the west end of Station Bridge.

THE BATHURST COMPANY'S HOMES, c. 1942

One of the biggest building booms in Bathurst's history was in 1920. That was the year that the Bathurst Co. began construction of their company homes. Most of these homes have since been torn down or removed. Only a few along Murray Avenue remain. The large homes seen on Pine Avenue in the above photo are also gone. They were erected in 1916. The homes in the foreground were removed in 1971 to make way for a mill parking lot. Two landmarks seen in this interesting photo, probably taken in the early 1940s are the arena, which was torn down in 1998, and the standpipe which is no longer in use but still standing.

BATHURST MILL SEEN FROM CN OVERPASS, C. 1922

This unique photo of the Bathurst Company Mill and company houses was taken shortly after the dwellings were constructed in 1920. The view is from the Murray Avenue CN overpass, which was constructed around 1922, looking east is a much altered landscape today. The houses are gone and the mill has, for the most part, been replaced with a newer modern structure, and the railway tracks leading to the right are gone. The water tank which can be seen towering over the mill fell down on November 13th, 1946. The tank crashed to the ground between two buildings at 5:00 P.M. in the evening, mere seconds after a group of men had walked through the alleyway leaving work. One worker, Al Ruddock, a company bricklayer who remained behind to finish up his job, was soaked by the tidal wave from the exploding tank but was otherwise unhurt. Water also gushed through the windows of the plant, damaging machinery.

A.E. MCLEAN'S "FLYING MACHINE" AT YOUGHALL BEACH

In July of 1929, A.E. McLean of the Bathurst Company acquired a "flying machine" and had it flown to his summer home at Youghall Beach. The *Tiger Moth* was flown from Montreal by an experienced pilot, and the seven-hour flight was without incident—up until the plane landed on the beach. The machine hit a stump partially buried in the sand and a wheel was torn off. A mechanic was flown in from Saint John to perform the necessary repairs and install pontoons for smoother landing on the bay. In the above photograph, Mr. McLean's airplane is shown resting on a special runway, designed to carry the airplane from the water to a hangar that was located on the property. The McLean home, which can be seen in the background, no longer exists.

A Grand Celebration

Bathurst has always been at the forefront of embracing new technology and industry. Its citizenry was also ready to celebrate milestones in these areas. The successful completion of the "Mighty Enterprise" of the Trans-Atlantic telegraph cable from the Old World to New, along the bed of the vast Atlantic Ocean was cause for great festivity from Bathurst residents. A huge extravaganza was held in Bathurst on September 1, 1858, to mark the occasion with much spirit and display.

The program of events for the day were printed in the local newspaper: 6:00 A.M., twenty-one guns fired from the wharf of Ferguson Rankin & Co. to usher in the day; 9:30 A.M, a boat race for four-oared gigs, a distance of 1-1/2 miles; 10:30 A.M., a canoe race over a two-and-a-half-mile course; noon, a twenty-one-gun salute was again fired. At 3:00 P.M., a horse race in the Village of St. Peters, ten horses entered and Dr. Bishop's black horse, Knickerbocker, was declared the winner after three gruelling hours; and at 6:30 P.M., a foot race. It was declared that "the number of persons that collected together to witness and participate in these amusements and trials of strength, speed, and skill, exceeded anything ever before seen in this comparatively thinly populated country." It was estimated that not less than one thousand persons were present.

As soon as night had fairly dropped her mantle on the harbour shore, the public offices, post office, telegraph, treasury, and registry, and several shops and dwelling houses were brightly illuminated. A great procession then made its way through the town. The handsome fire engine of the Ferguson Rankin & Co., decked with flowers and streamers, drawn by two horses, attended by upwards of fifty torches and preceded by a brass band, led the parade. The parade ended at a great bonfire in front of William End's house where the revelers gathered until 11:30 P.M before retiring to their homes, declaring, "It was the greatest day Gloucester ever witnessed."

In about 1786, James Sutherland, an Englishman of Scottish descent, married a handsome young lady of good family and sailed with her to America to make his future home in Boston. An episode soon followed that turned Sutherland into a New Brunswicker. It began in a Boston hotel, shortly after his arrival in that town. He became involved in a political discussion with an American citizen whose animosities from the American revolution had not subsided. In the heat of the argument, the Bostonian besmirched the British King's name. As Sutherland was a staunch Briton, the only reply he could give to such an insult was to knock the man down.

The consequences of such an encounter in those days was a challenge to a duel; a challenge Sutherland promptly accepted. The fight took place in a lonely spot outside the city and the Bostonian was killed.

As a result, Massachusetts was no longer a safe place for Sutherland. So, along with his wife and belongings, made his way to Saint John, arriving there in 1788. He remained in the port city for a year and then sailed to the Gulf of St. Lawrence and settled on the shores of the Nepisiguit Bay at Bathurst where he engaged himself in business and became a leading citizen in the village.

Sutherland obtained a large tract of land near Caron Point. It was leased for 999 years at a rental of "three pepper corns a year." The grant allowed that everything on the land, in the air, and in the forest belonged to the grantee.

In 1818, the Sutherlands learned that Hugh Munro of Bathurst, a ruthless magistrate, was preparing a case in Fredericton to take over their land. Munro claimed that the land clearing quote stipulated in the grant had not been fulfilled.

His twenty-year-old daughter Charlotte Sutherland, fearing that the grant might be rescinded, snowshoed to Fredericton with her sixteen-year-old brother in a record eight days to petition the governor to credit improvements to the grant to her lease requirements. The "improvements" included a dam fifteen feet high and eight feet wide on the river crossing the granted land. Though the dam had been built by beavers, her petition was granted.

As their epic journey took place in midwinter it was perilous. They followed the course of rivers and trails through the woods to reach their destination. With no houses between Bathurst and the Miramichi, the two slept in the open or under spruce boughs at night. Between Newcastle and Fredericton they occasionally found lodging in farmhouses or taverns.

The Sutherlands successfully defended their title to the land grant, which exists to this day.

NORTHERN MACHINE WORKS GARAGE, ON WATER STREET

In May 1919, Messrs. Alfred E. Eddy and Mearle Smith established Northern Machine Works Garage, advertising oxy-acetylene welding and general black-smithing. The partners were well-equipped to handle all kinds of equipment repairs and rebuilding. Mr. Eddy spent many years in Philadelphia where he became an expert in everything pertaining to gas engines and electricity. Mr. Smith was a blacksmith of unusual ability. The building, located on Water Street, where the city garage is today, was equipped with lathes, drills, and welders all necessary to the trade. Power for the equipment was supplied by a gasoline engine, but the partners indicated they were soon expecting to switch to electricity, "that strange and subtle fluid." In 1921, Mr. Smith bought out his partner, quit motor car work, and con-fined his activities to general machine work, oxy-acetylene welding, and electric welding. By 1930, he had a new steel and concrete machine shop that was expanded many times in the subsequent years. Remaining true to his profession as a smith and machinist, he began specializing in the manufacture of snow plows and dozer blades. Mearle Smith was born at Salmon Beach in 1893. At the age of fifteen, he went to work at the Bathurst Iron Mines as an apprentice Blacksmith. He also applied his trade in the construction of the Bathurst Pulp Mill in 1914.

ELHATTON'S CARRAGE AND UNDERTAKING LTD., C. 1890

Elhatton is a name that has been identified longer than most with the business and commercial life of Bathurst, and of New Brunswick, for that matter. It was in the mid-1800s that the Peter Elhatton Carriage and Undertaking Ltd. was established at the same St. George Street location occupied today by its successor, Elhatton's Funeral Home Ltd. The firm's history is a very interesting one. The above photograph (circa 1890) was taken when the carriage and sleigh trade was at its height. The adult figure in the foreground is Peter Elhatton, the company's founder. Peter Elhatton, born in County Tyrone, Ireland, emigrated to Canada with his father at the age of twelve in 1843 and settled in Pokeshaw. In 1852, he came to Bathurst and served a seven-year apprenticeship in the carriage trade as a wheelwright with a man named Lockart. When the manufacturing business was at its peak, two blacksmiths, three carpenters, two painters and four or five helpers were employed, a sizeable staff for that era. They produced driving wagons (known throughout Gloucester County as the Hatton Wagon, and some of which remain in existence), Phaeton buggies, sleighs, truck wagons, and slovens. In the meantime, Elhatton's went further into the funeral director's field and coffins were also manufactured in their plant. Three types of hearses were used in those early days. In the summer, it was a high black model drawn by a team of matching black horses; in the winter was exchanged for a lower one on the bobsleds for easier manoeuvering in the deep snow. A white hearse also equipped with bobsleds was used for children's funerals. Peter Elhatton died in 1921 and he was succeeded in the business by a partnership involving his sons Fred and Frank. Automobiles then became the order of the day and horse-drawn vehicles gradually faded into obsolescence, so by 1927 Elhatton's concentrated almost entirely on funeral service. In 1930, at the height of the Depression, the front portion of the old carriage building was torn down and replaced with a brick structure that still serves today as a funeral home.

J.A. PINAULT, UNDERTAKER ON ST. PATRICK STREET

J.A. Pinault was an undertaker and funeral director in the late 1800s and early part of the twentieth century. An advertisement for his services guaranteed "prompt and satisfactory service with modern hearses and equipment." His business was located on St. Patrick Street, opposite A.T. Hintons Store. His advertisements also stated that he operated "a black hearse for adults and a white hearse for children" and had "caskets of all kinds at reasonable prices." The caskets were manufactured by a local craftsman, Peter Elhatton.

Chapter 5

The Harnessing of the Great Falls

THE GRAND FALLS POWER STATION
NEARING COMPLETION C. 1925

The muffled roar of a mighty cataract that poured its waters through a rocky gorge and over a steep precipice for many centuries was silenced by a huge power development in 1926.

The Great Falls power dam and hydro-electric development was completed in that year at a cost of over three million dollars. The huge project was begun in 1919 and by 1921 the dam was completed. The task of harnessing the power of the Great Falls was a major undertaking. The cataract powered through a canyon of solid granite and dropped over one hundred feet into a gorge.

Four hundred men toiled for a year and a half to build the dam and the project consumed two-hundred-and-fifty carloads of cement, two hundred carloads of steel, and five thousand carloads of sand and gravel. It required over one hundred rail cars to transport machinery and equipment to the site by rail. A small town sprung up at the site of the falls and everything had to be brought in by rail to supply the people living there.

Even new rails had to be laid down on the Northern New Brunswick and Seaboard Railway to replace those lifted and used as war material during the First World War that had just ended. The project was built with difficulties in other areas as well. In 1894 the Great Falls Water Power and Boom Co. acquired the interests in the falls from the Dominion of Canada which owned the northeast bank of the river at Grand Falls, having acquired it for military purposes before confederation.

In 1905 a rival company, The Grand Falls Power Co., obtained the interests of the Southwest bank from the Province of New Brunswick. A deadlock between these two companies prevented any development of the falls until 1912 when the Great Falls Co. acquired the properties of its rival.

Shortly thereafter the International Paper Co. obtained a two-third interest in the new company and development seemed certain—but was interrupted again by the outbreak of World War One. Following the war, a period of inflation followed by a severe depression again postponed the project.

To add to the difficulties there were five political entities involved in the development: the Dominion of Canada, the United States of America, the Province of New Brunswick, the State of Maine, and the Province of Quebec. On August 10th of 1926, New Brunswick Premier J.B. Baxter detonated a sharp explosion that signalled the formal commencement of hydro-electric power from the development to the Bathurst Company Pulp and paper mill located downstream and the homes and businesses in the town. The ceremony was attended by almost the entire population of Bathurst as well as visitors who came by special charter train from all parts of New Brunswick and Maine.

The Great Falls on the Nepisiguit River prior to the construction of the power dam.

THE
TETAGOUCHE
FALLS POWER
DAM
c. 1910

RIGHT

POWER STATION AT GRAND FALLS c. 1926

The power station at Great Falls, sixteen miles upriver from Bathurst.

Light and Water come to Bathurst

Until the early part of the twentieth century, the people of Bathurst drew their water from public wells and lit their homes with oil lamps and candles. When travelling by night, they lit their way with hand held lanterns. No street lights existed until about 1900 when a Bathurst lawyer, George C. Gilbert, installed oil lamps at street corners at his own expense. He purchased one dozen tin lamps and had them attached to poles at each street corner. He also paid for the services of someone to fill and light them each night.

The oil street lamps remained in use until 1904 when John P. Leger formed the Bathurst Electric and Water Power Company and erected a hydro-electric plant at Tetagouche River Falls to supply the town with electricity.

In 1880, the St. Peter's Village Water Company was incorporated and a system of water supply pipes were installed to convey water to the village from springs in the hills west of the railway tracks. However, it was not until 1915 that a water and sewer system was installed that could pump water to individual homes. The source of supply was Carter's Brook and a 405,000 gallon stand pipe was erected in the town to hold the water that was pumped from a reservoir located near Golf Street.

A view of the Bathurst pump house and water reservoir from Golf Street hill c. 1940.

Telephones

As the great fire of 1914 raged through the streets of Bathurst, wiping out a complete town block, Reginald Boss saw his life's dreams and accomplishments go up in flames.

Seated in an express wagon with a telephone switchboard and other central office equipment piled in the back, Mr. Boss and his wife watched the walls of their once beautiful home crumble to the ground as flames consumed it.

Reginald Boss had sacrificed practically all of his personal belongings in order to maintain telephone service as long as possible as fire ravaged the buildings around him and finally his home, which housed the Bathurst telephone exchange.

In less than two hours, Mr. Boss had secured temporary quarters for his telephone exchange in the Robertson Building on Water Street. Equipment was moved in and the telephones were back in service before the day was through. It was this determination and hard work that made him one of Bathurst's leading industrialists.

Reginald Boss was born into a mercantile family in 1865. His father Charles ran a general store in Bathurst dealing in groceries, dry goods, and hardware; he also ran a brickyard and a factory that made refrigerators. The Boss freezer was a popular trademark in Bathurst.

At an early age, Reginald Boss took an interest in telephone transmission, which was then in its infancy. He first experimented with two tin cans as transmitters and a tightly drawn string as a line. He later improved the device by using two tin drums over which he stretched a thin piece of sheepskin and from a button sewn in the center of the skin of each instrument he strung a bare copper wire. This means of communication proved so satisfactory that he installed the device in his family home and one in his father's place of business. He later extended a line to the post office.

The first standard telephones were installed in Bathurst in 1885 when the Bell Telephone Company built a ground line between the Intercolonial Railway Station in the Bathurst Village and the Bathurst-Caraquet railway station in East Bathurst, a distance of two-and-a-half miles.

Reginald Boss was engaged by the company to look after the maintenance of the line and sub-stations. This set him on his career in the telephone exchange business. In 1890, he constructed a telephone line from the store of Louis Poirier of Caraquet to his home, a distance of two miles. In 1891 he installed three miles of telephone line connecting the stores of Robert Young and sons of Tracadie, general merchants and exporters of fish. In 1892 he put down a ground cable for the Dominion Government connecting the islands of Miscou and Shippegan to the mainland. This was his first experience in laying a submarine cable.

Mr. Boss's enterprise, the Gloucester Telephone Company, was purchased by the Central Telephone Company in 1906 and he was appointed general manager of the new firm. In May of that same year work began, running a telephone toll line from Bathurst to Newcastle. In 1907 the Central Telephone Company and the New Brunswick Telephone Company amalgamated and Mr. Boss stayed on as their local manager.

Mr. Boss also served as district superintendent of the New Brunswick Telephone Company. Only one year after the fire of 1914 Mr. Boss rebuilt a splendid new home to the same exact architectural design as his previous one and at the same location on St. George Street. The telephone exchange was moved into the new building where it remained until 1939.

During his years in the telephone business, Mr. Boss had many other interests: he was registrar of births, marriages and deaths for Gloucester County and he was an organist at the Anglican Church. He also conducted a business on Water Street dealing with electrical appliances, telephones, bicycles, sewing machines, and pianos. In his spare time, he made bricks at his backyard in the Village.

The remains of the Bathurst Telephone Exchange after the great fire of 1914.

NEW BATHURST TELEPHONE EXCHANGE

The New Bathurst Telephone Exchange rises from the ashes of its predecessor.

THE NEW TELEPHONE EXCHANGE BUILDING

A view of King Avenue looking north. The third telephone exchange building shown at the left was erected in 1938 by the New Brunswick Telephone Company and still serves the telephone company today.

Chapter 6

Mills, Mining, and Lumbering

**THE THIRD EDITION OF THE GEORGE EDDY MILL
BUILT IN 1925.**

Mills

George Samuel Eddy was born in 1863 in the small hamlet of New Bandon, near Bathurst. He was the son of an Irish immigrant, Robert Eddy, who came from Bandon, Ireland. He came to New Brunswick in 1823 and founded the community of New Bandon in honor of the place of his birth.

In 1895 George Eddy established a planing mill at Bathurst. The mill operated under many disadvantages as the machinery and equipment were antiquated and Mr. Eddy's financial resources were limited. However, he was a tireless worker and he managed to make a success of the venture. But just as he was beginning to get through his industrial difficulties, the plant, along with huge piles of valuable lumber, were destroyed by a fire.

Undismayed, Mr. Eddy struggled on, he built a bigger and better woodworking factory. The plant ran successfully until 1925 when once more disaster struck and the factory again went up in flames. The mill was rebuilt and back in operation within three months—a notable achievement considering it was seventy-three years ago.

SECOND MILL BY GEORGE EDDY

A second mill built by George Eddy burned in 1925. The flour and feed mill shown at the left of the photograph was built in 1916. At the time it was built, the forty-barrel mill housed the most up-to-date milling equipment available.

GLOUCESTER MILL BEFORE THE 1924 FIRE It was Sunday, May 24 in 1924 when the Gloucester Lumber and Trading Company No.1 mill went up in flames. The large wooden structure was located on Black Street, about where the oil tanks are today. As shown in the accompanying photograph, the view was substantially different from what we see today. The Burns and Adams mill can be seen on the east side of the river and lumber is piled on the full length of the shoreline. A tugboat sits in the harbour while another one is tied up at a wharf to the right of the mill. The wharf and equipment seen at the right of the photo is what remained of Cunard's Shipbuilding Enterprise.

THE OLD MILL, BEFORE 1898 In this photo, the old mill is seen again at the left, with a view of Black Street (lower Main Street) and the East Bathurst Bridge as seen from the hill near St. John Street. It was taken before 1898, as a new iron span bridge was constructed over the Nepisiguit River that year. Also notable, by its absence, is the pulp mill which was not constructed until 1914. The vacant land was part of the Cunard farm and was acquired by the Bathurst Company when they built the mill.

No. 1 MILL, IN WEST BATHURST

The Bathurst Lumber Company's No. 1 mill shown here was located in West Bathurst at a site where Canadian Tire is now situated. The mill was constructed around 1909 and operated until about 1930 when production ceased.

STACEY'S MILL, ON RIVERSIDE DRIVE

Stacey's Mill and homestead was located on the bank of the basin on Riverside Drive, near Golf Street.

GLOUCESTER MILL ON LOWER WATER ST. Piles of lumber and firewood line the road leading to the Gloucester Lumber and Trading Company mill on Lower Water Street.

JOHN FERGUSON'S SECOND MILL John Ferguson's second mill was built in the mid-1800s. The offices and warehouses shown were located near the West Bathurst Wharf. It was acquired by the Bathurst Lumber Company in 1905 and used as offices and warehouses for their woodlands division until early 1980s.

MILLS BURNS IN 1908, 1915

On March 31, 1908, the Bathurst Lumber Company mill in West Bathurst went up in flames. Though it remains uncertain, the fire was most likely the result of a spark from the huge furnace that powered the steam plant. The conflagration threatened the entire village until a shift in the wind saved the community from certain destruction. The mill, built by the Ferguson Rankin Company only a few years earlier, was a total loss. The mill was located at the present site of the sewage filtration plant at the end of Riverside Drive. On September 29 of 1915, fire struck the West Bathurst mill of the Bathurst Lumber Company again. Millions of feet of dry lumber piled on the company's dockyard went up in flames. A sea of flames stretched for half a mile along the great road to Restigouche (St. Peter Avenue) as pile after pile of seasoned lumber went up in flames. It was reported that upwards of fifteen million feet of lumber was destroyed in the conflagration. Although the company wharf was badly damaged, the mill was saved.

LUMBER YARDS ON ST. PETER AVENUE, c. 1920

TOP RIGHT

This is what a large section of St. Peter Avenue looked like circa 1920 when this photograph was taken. Shown here are the lumber yards of the Bathurst Lumber Company which operated a saw and planing mill that spanned both sides of the avenue. Today the area is a labyrinth of shopping malls, stores, and service stations.

THE FINISHING MILL ON ST. PETER AVENUE, c. 1920

BOTTOM RIGHT

The Bathurst Lumber Company finishing mill was situated on the south side of St. Peter Avenue, where Tim Horton's Doughnut shop is located today. It was built at the beginning of the twentieth century and operated into the 1930s. The unique feature of this mill was a large pipe that ran across the highway some 1,000 feet to the Company's No. 1 mill, situated on the shore of the bay. It carried shavings to fire the furnaces of the No. 1 mill. The above photograph, probably taken in the early 1920s, shows St. Peter Avenue as a ditched, muddy road back then.

LUMBER YARD (ABOVE) AND FINISHING MILL (BELOW) ON ST. PETER AVENUE

ADAMS BURNS MILL, c. 1886

The Adams Burns Company Mill circa 1886. The mill was located on the eastern side of the mouth of the Nepisiguit River and operated until it was purchased by the Bathurst Lumber Company in 1912.

B Lbr Co Mill No 2   Bathurst N.B.   291

COMPANY'S No. 2 MILL, 1920

The Bathurst Lumber Company Mill No. 2 operated on the east bank of the Nepisiguit River and was originally owned by the Adams Burns and Co. The above photograph was taken in 1920 and shows the plant in full production.

The schooners, *Margaret Thomas* and *Thealine* docked at the Bathurst Lumber Company's No. 1 wharf in West Bathurst in 1920.

GRIST AND
CARDING
MILL ON
THE TETA-
GOUCHE

This early photograph shows a grist and carding mill on the Tetagouche River. The mill stood approximately where the Tetagouche River Bridge leading to North Tetagouche stands today. The photo was taken in the nineteenth century, before there was any bridge at all spanning the river. Around the mid-1800s, a log structure known as Brown's Mill Dam Bridge was built near the site. It was replaced in 1916 by the steel bridge that is still there. Since the earliest days in Bathurst, there was a need for mills to grind wheat, buckwheat, and corn. As well, carding, lumber, and shingle mills were also common. One of the earliest mills was erected on the top of the Village Hill and was powered by a windmill. Around the mid-eighteenth century, hydro power was more commonly used to run these mills. In fact, almost every river that ran through the area had a mill of some sort located on its shores. By 1908, the waters of the Tetagouche River were harnessed to produce electricity, which in turn was also used to power mills in Bathurst.

Mining

Mining has a long history in Bathurst dating back to the early years of the nineteenth century. In 1840 Manganese—a rare earth metal—was discovered on the Tetagouche and Peters Rivers. William Stevens and Joseph Kent engaged in Manganese mining for some time at Tetagouche. Their endeavour had varying successes and their first shipment was lost when the sailing ship it was being transported to Europe on went down in the Atlantic Ocean.

Copper deposits were found on the Nepisiguit River in 1837 and the Gloucester Mining Company was formed to mine the area. The company spent large amounts of money on the mine and shipped large quantities of ore to England without renumeration.

Limestone was found in great abundance at Elm Tree, located fifteen miles west of Bathurst. A geological survey in 1844 by a Dr. Gesner stated that the area also contained large deposits of marble. Dr. Gesner's assessment of the marble was that "the prevailing color of the marble is white which graduates into buff colored green and gray." He went on to suggest that machinery might be erected and a marble sawed and polished which would "equal in beauty and quality of any other part of the world."

In 1880 a vein was discovered on the north branch of the Nigadoo River, carrying zinc, lead, and silver. In 1897 William Hussey of Big River discovered Iron deposits in the Austin Brook area and the Austin Brook Iron Mine was formed in 1903. The mine was in production until 1913 and operated under the name of Drummond Mines Limited.

After the First World War began there was a great demand for iron to build war machinery. The Dominion Steel and Coal Company obtained the rights to operate the property from the Canadian Iron Industries, who held the lease, and re-opened the mine. Other ore discoveries attracted Noranda, Anadonda, and O'Brien Gold Mines to the area.

**DRUMMOND
MINE** The Drummond Mine concentrator and ramp leading to the ore crusher.

**THE IRON
HIGHWAY** The Northern New Brunswick and Seaboard Railway line winds its way past the
office building and accommodations at the Drummond Iron Mines.

Lumbering

The cold raw power of a mighty, ice-filled river in a spring flood is an awesome thing. Only those who have seen its unleashed power, when suddenly released from three days of confinement behind ten million feet of logs and 25,000 cords of eight foot pulpwood, can sense the horrendous energy of such a force.

These are the words of Richard Edwin Elliott who worked on a river drive down the Nepisiguit in 1928. Elliott was only seventeen years old at the time and he wrote of his experience in later years.

Young Richard Elliott was given the job of sacking along the rear of the drive, breaking jams, and pulling wings off the river banks. This was cold, wet, dangerous work and he was required at times to carry a dozen sticks of dynamite along with blasting caps in a sack on his back as he trudged along the riverbank in knee deep snow with fallen trees and slippery rocks for footing.

Nineteen twenty eight witnessed one of the biggest log jams on the river—it was nearly three miles long and it took three days to release it with dynamite and peaveys. When the jam finally gave way it exploded with such force that logs three feet in diameter were snapped in two while others were thrown thirty feet into the air. Elliott reported that: "the noise was deafening, like the roar of a dozen freight trains travelling at full throttle."

As the river raged and tore into the log jam the sackers scurried toward the safety of the riverbank with death only split seconds behind them. The average loss on the Nepisiguit drive due to accidents was three men a year. All along the portage road there were wooden crosses spiked to trees to mark the points where men had been killed or drowned.

One of the worst places on the river was the Narrows—a quarter-mile stretch of the Nepisiguit extending through a canyon of rock cliffs more than fifty-feet high. As water rushed through this narrow gorge it caused huge rapids and eddies as it roared over and around huge boulders in the passage. Elliott recounted the frightening experience of going through the rapids of the Narrows during his days on the drive in the spring of 1928.

That year they ran four boats through the narrows and he volunteered to ride in one of them. He described his harrowing experience as follows:

The boat began to pick up speed, slowly at first, and then with an ever increasing tempo sucking the boat into the jaws of the gorge. The cliffs seemed to reach into the skies for ever and the river was squeezed into a slit which was half wide enough. The roar became rapidly louder and closer. It was a terrifying sound. As if grasped by some unseen hand the boat suddenly leapt forward. At first it was a matter of great speed and then we hit the big backward bending roller. The bowman rose until he was flat out on his back right above me and then he went down until I was looking along his back right under my boots. There were a series of these and then came a stretch of fast, black water. We came into this off a high roller and the acceleration was magnificent. The force of our descent and the sudden forward motion of the boat propelled us at frightening speed and we went by so fast that water which was four to five inches above the gunwales of the boat has no time to fall in because we passed too quickly. The roar of the rushing water against the confining walls had become so great that all other sounds were obliterated. There were more rollers, more fast water, and then we were out onto the relatively calm waters of the river where it widened out below the gorge.

A log jam at Grand Falls on the Nepisiguit.

Life in the Lumber Camps

L ife in the lumber camps was hard, lonely, and monotonous during the great lumbering days of twentieth century. Men journeyed "up-river," a four-day journey for some, by horse and sled or wagon. They then spent the winter months in a wood cutting camp putting in long hours of work risking injury or even death for eight or ten dollars a month; most of which was owed to the company store before they even received it. Despite the discomforts of life in the woods there was no lack of men willing and eager to return to the camps year after year.

A wood cutting operation usually consisted of the main camp and a hovel for the horses. The main camp was quite often no more than a hovel itself, a shack with pine boughs for a bed. Some operations had a cook house with an open fireplace used for cooking. The main camp housed up to fifty men and was usually well ventilated; a necessity with the luxury of a shower or bathtub non existent.

In 1870 the cost of putting up a camp, storehouse and hovel for fifty men was $300. Each wood cutting outfit had a variety of men doing different jobs; at the top of the list was the boss. Next, a man of great influence—the cook. Among the other job descriptions were choppers, swampers, barkers, loaders, and teamsters all necessary to fell the big trees and get them to the river in time for the drive.

Work began before daybreak and the men only returned to camp at dusk. After supper, which consisted mostly of salt pork, bread, beans, and molasses, the men spent a few hours playing cards, whittling, pipe smoking, singing, and storytelling. The oil lights were extinguished at 9:00 P.M. and the men retired to their bunks in anticipation of another long day in the woods come daybreak.

In the early 1800s, drunkenness was prevalent among woods workers. Along with barrels of salt pork, hogsheads of rum were standard among the cook's provisions. One observer remarked that, "Liquor flowed as freely as the waters which bore their logs to the mills." Because of the dangers it wrought, alcohol was banned from all camps by 1860. The men, deprived of a drink of spirits for the months they spent at camp, made up for it when they were paid and many of them "raised hell" when they came into town.

In April of 1882 a group of woodsmen arrived in Bathurst with their winters wages in their pockets and devilment on their minds. The citizens of the town were not amused and the local newspaper carried the following report in that week's issue:

Saturday last the town was entirely delivered into the hands of pugilistic element. A large number of woodsmen came in and a great number imbibed rather freely after their winter's exile. The result was free fights in almost every corner of the town and as usual our police officers were conspicuous by their absence. Such an amount of brawling had not been seen in our town since the time of railway construction.

Although some incidents of rowdiness both in town and in the camps were recorded, woodsmen for the most part were a hard working lot who just wanted a little fun and merriment on occasions.

A description of the woodsman offered by one John McGregor in 1828 seems a little extreme but serves to illustrate what was written about these men back in the early years of lumbering:

> Their moral character, with few exceptions, is dishonest and worthless. I believe there are few people in the world on whose promises less faith can be placed than that of the lumberer….In New Brunswick…the epithet "lumberer" is considered synonymous with a character of

WORKING AT THE POPPLE CAMP, MID-1930S

A group of equine and human workers pose for a photographer at the lumbering camp at Popple back in the mid-1930s. Those were the depression years and work was scarce back then. Both men and horses worked long hours, for small pay but were fortunate to have employment at all. Those workers identified in the picture are: Walter Glidden, Ernest Pentland, Duncan Campbell and Gordon Graham.

spendthrift habits, and villainous and vagabond principles. After selling and delivering up their rafts, they pass some weeks in idle indulgence, drinking, smoking, and dashing off, in a long coat, flashy waistcoat and trousers, Wellington or Hessian boots, a handkerchief of many colours round the neck, a watch with a long tinsel chain and numberless brass seals, and an umbrella.

McGregor's view of the woodsmen was strongly criticized at the time and he was deemed to be as "unfit to write history as to make it."

Considering the tough times, hard work, and isolated conditions these men worked in, all for small pay, it is small wonder that they went on a spree when the logs reached the mill. Like the lives of those men who moiled for gold, fished the seas, or farmed the land in days of old, the life of the woodsman has also been immortalized in stories, songs and poems. One such poem, penned by an unknown author appeared in an old edition of *The Northern Light* entitled "The Lumberjack":

O' a restless soul is the lumberjack:
Through the length and breadth of the old North Shore.
He harken to the woodland's majestic lure
From country and hamlet humble abode
Autumn calls him to the balsam road.
When the needles turn on the tamarack tree,
And the first frost sparkles like a soul set free,
Then from Big River and Tetgagouche.
He's up and away and he's off to the bush.

O, he's young and he's old is the lumberjack:
A young lad weary of dull town days
With a roving fancy and a distant gaze--
Who quits his companions as his whole heart fills
With the pain-sharp beauty of the hardwood hills;
Or a farmer, father now of tall grown sons,
Whose restless feet take him once again
To that peaceful and hurryless world of men...

Chapter 7

Sports of Bathurst

FIRE DEPARTMENT TRACK AND FIELD CHAMPS, 1944

The above photo shows the 1944 Bathurst Power and Paper Fire Department track and field team which won top honors in the annual North Shore Fireman's sports and field day that year. The tournament was staged in Bathurst and hosted teams from around the province. Front row, left to right, Rudolph White and John Vienneau. Second row: A.J. Roy, Pius Roy, Raymond Audet, Joseph Noel, and Douglas Shirley. Third row: Fire Chief R.M. Young, George Beaulieu, Emile Ouellette, Vincent Lavigne, and assistant fire chief A. Ray Morrison. In the centre of the group is the team mascot, Jumbo. Also pictured are the Fred MacKay Memorial Shield, awarded annually to the team with the greatest number of points, and the cup for the hose department contest.

Horse racing

A 1927 Victoria Day Holiday race at the Bathurst Race Track serves as an excellent example of the excitement a day at the races held. Over one thousand spectators lined the rails surrounding the track to watch the card of events that day—a three minute trot or pace; a free for all—a race in which horses from any class could enter; a field of trotters and the most exciting event on the card: saddle racing with five horses entered. A.E. McLean, Geo. A. Schryer, Thomas Magson, Frank Baldwin, and Willie Silva charged from the gate on their horses and as they rounded the first turn, Schryer fell from his mount when his saddle strap broke. It was a stirring spectacle with the rider scrambling for safety as his horse continued the race running neck and neck with the lead horse. To add to the drama, nine-year-old Gilbert Hachey suddenly ran onto the track directly in front of the horses and fell under their hooves. In the meantime one of the spectators, overcome with the excitement, took a weak turn and fell unconscious to the ground! Four races were on the card that day and a purse of $140 was awarded. A light-heavyweight boxing match was also staged at the track that day. Gordon Hodgons and Freeman Watson fought for a $10 purse.

Bathurst Race Track was established in 1900 on the present site of the Forest Glen Subdivision off Sunset Dr. Although horse racing dates back to Bathurst's earliest days when, in 1858, Dr. Samual Bishop raced his black horse Knickerbocker.

In its heyday, the 1930s and '40s, the racing complex comprised the railed track, grandstand and stables which eventually crumbled or burned. Familiar names connected with the sport during these years, either as horse owners, drivers or officials included W.G. Fenwick, Gilchrist MacDonald, Al. O'Donnell, S.P. (Syd.) Vienneau, Eddie Shirley, Warren Dempsey, Eddie Chiasson, B.C. Mullins, and W.F. Sullivan.

James Kenny, a prominent businessman, lumberman, contractor, and farmer of his era, was among those most closely identified with harness racing here and elsewhere for many years. He owned and drove among others Marvin Brooks, a pacer with a mark of 2.05, Awlydale and Dr. Jenkins. These horses raced in Chatham, Campbellton, and Mont Joli. The jockeys included Bob Morrison and Toby Lavigne, while Stan Noel transported the steeds from track to track.

In the 1940s, Queenie O'Neil, another Jim Kenny pacer, raced in Chatham, Buctouche and Sackville. In the late 1950s and and 1960s, William Morrison travelled the circuit with Gentleman J.R. and Labour Day.

SILK GIRL SETS TRACK RECORD, 1940

Silk Girl, a grey trotter owned by Dr. L.D. Densmore and driven by Bob Morrison reaches the finish line to set a record of 2.17 at Bathurst Race Track, which was never bettered. Coming in close behind is Jim Kenny's trotter, Barn Watts, with Ken Love in the seat. This particular mid-summer 1940 event was among the last staged on the local scene where the sport was on the wane and soon to die altogether. Lining the rails are Second World War troops here in connection with a Victory Bond promotion.

Early history of Baseball in Bathurst

The first record of a game of baseball being played by a Bathurst team was in 1893 when a group of players travelled to the Miramichi to take on the Chatham team. The game was played in the horse racing park. By 1896 regularly scheduled games were underway. The West Bathurst Grammar School went against the Bathurst Grammar School and regular games were played in Market Square (near the Cathedral).

P.J. Veniot, Joe Bertin, and Don Connolly were considered to be the best sluggers of the era and oftentimes hit the ball over the Cathedral Church or down into the marsh—on many occasions losing the ball.

Practically all the equipment used was hand-made. A peavey handle was used for a bat, until Thomas Gammon turned out bats for the boys in his wood-working shop. (He also made wooden curling stones). A small rubber ball or piece of cork wound with twine, covered with leather by John Doucet, a shoemaker, was the only type of ball used for years. Leather mitts were hand-made by another shoemaker by the name of Tom Cantry, Sr. The most famous piece of equipment of all was a breast protector made by Eddie Melanson using leather and rubber and inflated by air. The air escaped so rapidly that games were frequently held up while the breast protector was pumped up.

During World War One, only the odd exhibition game was played, however, in the years after the war five local teams were playing frequently and baseball was enjoying a large following in Bathurst. In 1939 when war broke out again, many of the players left for service overseas and the game again fell into a slump.

The older players who stayed behind formed a softball league that lasted until 1950 when baseball was brought back to the town with the formation of Little League.

BATHURST'S BOYS OF SUMMER, 1911

In 1910, Gerald Comeau and Leonard Veniot organized a baseball league. They played their local games in the Catholic Church Park and in 1911 at Flannerys Point, where the photo at right was taken. Shown in the front are Gerald Comeau (left) and J. Leonard Veniot. Middle row, from left: Aurele Landry, J.E. Connolly, George Duval and Arthur Gammon. Back: Oswald Melanson, Arthur Lavigne, Ernest Rogers, Alfred DeGrace, and Harold Kent.

Curling in Bathurst dates back to 1883

The game of curling began in the fall of 1883 in Bathurst and "scratch" games were played on the ice of the harbour. Enthusiasm for the game caught on fast and the first indoor sheet of ice was prepared in a skating rink erected in 1884 by Edward D. Bassett. The rink was located on Water Street about where the Farmers Market is today.

The following year, Bassett built a curling ring with two sheets of ice adjoining a skating rink on the property now occupied by Elhatton's Funeral Home on St. George Street.

The Bassett Rink fell into disrepair and a group of curlers built a new two-sheet rink in 1889 again on Water Street, on the present site of the Kent Theatre building. This rink burned down in 1891 and a new one-sheet rink was immediately built only to collapse shortly after from an unusually heavy snowfall that built-up on the roof. Because of the loss of the rink the game was disrupted until 1907, when curling again resumed, this time on an outdoor rink at Kent's pond.

In 1909, a combined curling and skating rink was built on St. Andrew Street where the present club now stands. Another interruption to the game came in 1913 when the building was used as a barracks during the Great War. Fire destroyed the rink in February of 1940 and plans were immediately drawn up to replace it and the present four-sheet rink was erected.

Hockey history in Bathurst

Ice hockey was introduced to Bathurst immediately after World War One by well known sports figures Otho and George Schryer, Chap Veniot, Father Roe McKenna, Gordon Moar, Eck McLean, and Red McLean. The first of many papermaker hockey teams—those sponsored by local papermaking companies—was organized in 1928 when a club from Bathurst represented the North Shore Hockey league. They were the first New Brunswick team to participate in the Allan Cup playoffs that year. Girls' hockey also flourished in Bathurst in the early years of the sport.

1927 NORTHERN N.B. CHAMPIONS The Bathurst hockey team of 1927 secured the Northern New Brunswick championship title, defeating the Newcastle Club 4-1 on home ice Friday, Feb. 10, 1928. The team then went on to play Saint John for the provincial series. In the first game, played in Saint John, the Bathurst team held the famed Saint John Fusiliers down so effectively they only scored one goal. It was conceded by all to be one of the finest displays of hockey ever seen in the province. More than four thousand spectators packed the Saint John Arena. The team returned home to a heroes' welcome and in addition to the admiration of the citizens of Bathurst, each player was presented with a silver cigarette lighter by Mr. F.P. Gatain, of Gatain's store and dance hall, as a souvenir . In the above photo, reproduced from a silver print, are, back row, left ot right: J. Barberie (manager), Glint Gammon, Reirdon Cripps, Eloi McKenna, Art Aubie, Dud James and H.D. Schryer (manager). Front row: Anslem Doucett, Danny Cripps, Ken Carroll, Blair Carroll, and Tracy Bond. Gerald (Peewee) Doucet is in front, holding the Northern New Brunswick League trophy.

HIGH SCHOOL HOCKEY WINNERS, 1947

The above photo was taken in 1947, and was featured in a 1948 edition of *The Northern Light*. It shows the Bathurst High School hockey team, provincial inter-scholastic finalists. Winners of the North Shore school title, the Red and Black lost to the strong Moncton High School team in a two-game, total-goal series that year, after winning the first game at home 6-4. Shown in front row, from left, are Jack Aube, goal; Boyd Melanson, centre; Westley Blanchard, team captain and defence; Kenneth Frenette, forward; and Chesley Hornibrook, sub-goal. Second row: Ev Doucet, coach; Jackie Blanchard, forward; Mathias Stever, forward; Norman Boudreau, forward; and Don Hinton, manager. Back: Wilfred Bevin, forward; Gregory Arseneau, defence; Robert Maher, forward; Morley Gammon, forward; and Lawrence Frigault, forward.

BATHURST PAPERMAKERS, c. 1920

Organized ice hockey was introduced to Bathurst in 1919 and quickly became one of the town's favorite games. Shortly thereafter, a group of local sports enthusiasts, lead by H.O. Schryer, organized the first of many professional papermaker hockey teams. The above photograph, taken around 1920, shows one of those early teams, possibly the very first. The players, wearing the familiar red, white and black uniforms, bring back memories of a time long ago when the teams played for fun, honor and the pleasure of the hometown crowd. Back then, there were no heated arenas or even artificial ice, let alone big salaries. Older hockey fans will remember with nostalgia those days of Bill O'Donnell's and Perley Dunn's "Hot Stove" leagues, the six-month residency rule, stand-up goalies, and the special train excursions to out-of-town games. There was no forward pass then, and the hook check and the pole check were all part of the game. Players like Dud James, David Crosby, Fred and Blair Carroll, Clint Gammon, and Bill Ryan will live on perpetually in the annals of hockey. In the above photo, seated left to right, are: Bernard Lavigne, goalie; Bill Ryan, forward; David Crosby, defence; Otho Schryer, defence; and Gordon Moar, goalie. Standing: Danny Cripps, forward; Riordon Cripps, defence; and John White, forward. The eight players with two spares comprised the entire team.

Hockey rink collapses under snow, 1920

Bathurst's hockey rink collapsed under the weight of snow after a huge storm on Saturday, February 6, 1920 just a few months after its completion. Industrialist Angus MacLean immediately undertook the task of constructing a new arena and a new structure was in place before the year was out. It served as Bathurst's only hockey ice surface until 1997. It was demolished a year later.

A new rink (above) was under construction within weeks after disaster struck the original building.

Chapter 8

Transportation in Bathurst

A VERY EARLY SNOWMOBILE — 1928 BUICK WITH SKIS

Rev. A.J. Allard, Parish priest in East Bathurst and founder of Allardville, poses with an early version of a snowmobile, a 1928 Buick Master Six Sedan with Caterpillar tracks and skis attached. The vehicle belonged to Bathurst Industrialist, Sir James Dunn who used it to travel to his camp on the Dunn Road in the Allardville area. This photograph was taken at the Dunn camp on March 11, 1930.

Railroads

In the golden age of railroading, all manner of goods and livestock were transported by train. Circuses travelled across the country by special trains and when they arrived at the station the whole menagerie was paraded through the streets to alert the townfolk of their arrival and give them a preview of the great show that was in store for them.

Harvest trains travelling west carried men to the Prairies to work in the wheat fields. Wild horses from the western prairies were shipped east in boxcars and caused great excitement at the train stations where they were unloaded. The animals were herded through the streets of Bathurst by mounted cowboys, who accompanied them from the west, to a corral on Main Street where they were sold to local farmers and woods operations.

When both World Wars broke out, young Bathurst men who went to war began their journey at the railway station as tearful families bade them goodbye. Their triumphant return after the war ended at the railway station amidst great jubilation by those who waited at home.

During the Depression years of the late 1920s and 1930s, jobless men rode the rods from coast to coast in search of work. On many occasions, hobos jumped off the boxcars at Bathurst to spend time in the town. A wooded area near Golf Street was a regular stop for many of the travelling gentry and it was known as the "Jungle" because of its rough and tumble atmosphere.

At the other end of the spectrum, dignitaries rode the rails in posh pullman cars. These special trains pulled into the Bathurst station on many occasions. In August of 1923, Lord Byng of Vimy, Canada's Governor General and Lady Byng drew a large crowd to the Bathurst station. In 1927, two special trains of twenty-one cars arrived in Bathurst carrying a large delegation of VIPs from Montreal and Toronto under the Auspices of *Le Devoir*, a Montreal newspaper. Henri Bourassa, the Quebec politician and journalist, was among the 250 notables who visited Bathurst that day.

One of the last whistle stops made by a politician was in the spring of 1957 when Lester B. Pearson passed through Bathurst on the Ocean Limited. Over 1,500 Gloucester County residents converged on the station to greet the National Liberal Party Leader as he made a campaign tour of the Maritimes by rail.

From the earliest days of travel by rail, trainwrecks were frequent and disastrous to both men and machines. Just one year after the Caraquet and Gulf Shore Railway Line was completed the greatest disaster in the history of railroading in the area occurred. Eight men were killed in that accident of 1887. A speeding I.C.R. Express train jumped the rails near Bathurst in 1898 crushing the fireman beneath it as it struck a ditch. In October of

1909, a head-on collision at Jacquet River killed two railway engineers and the express messenger. A southbound freight train met the northbound CN Freight Extra 3240 at Doucet's Crossing in West Bathurst in 1925. The head-on collision killed the engineer and fourteen horses.

In the fall of 1925, a model-T Ford was struck by a CN freight train as it pulled into Bathurst. The driver of the automobile and the brakeman of the locomotive were both killed.

REAPER PARTS ARRIVING BY TRAIN Today huge combines cut and thresh the seasons growth of grain in short order. But it was not always so easy. In olden times, the grain was cut by arm power with a reaping hook, then later a scythe. The grain was gathered and tied into sheathes by hand. The sheathes were then bundled in stooks and left in the fields to dry. The invention of the "reaper" was a great step forward. This horse-drawn contraption cut the grain and tied it into sheathes. When dry, the sheathes were stored in barns and then were later threshed. The farmers in this early photograph are starting for home after picking up reaper parts delivered by freight to the Bathurst train station. All of them are driving what were known as "Hatton" wagons, a brand name in wagons that were manufactured locally by Peter Elhatton. The reapers were assembled at someone's barn and all hands gathered to see the new machinery in operation. Back in 1878 horses were the main means of farm power and much grain was needed as feed. Home-grown wheat was also ground into flour at the grist mills.

BATHURST TRAIN STATION, 1913-1966

For two-thirds of the twentieth century this building served as a ticket office and waiting room for local train travellers. Erected in 1913, it remained as such until replaced in 1966. An earlier depot was destroyed by fire. Obviously more picturesque than the present structure, it occupied a site close to the location where Via Rail presently holds forth. Another striking contrast to the present scene at train time today is the lineup of horse-drawn hacks shown in the picture which, after depositing passengers, waited to pick up prospective guests for the local hostelries.

STEVE BRANCH ABOARD A HANDCAR, C. 1895

TOP RIGHT   At the turn of the century, Steve Branch was a section foreman on the Intercolonial rail line. His section was comprised of an area on Gloucester Junction main line. Mr. Branch and his crew worked six days a week repairing and maintaining that section of track. He is shown in the photo top right (circa 1895) on a handcar on the tracks of Gloucester Junction. The handcar was used to travel to work and to inspect the tracks for broken or loose rails and ties.

STEAM LOCOMOTIVE WAITING AT THE OLD TRAIN STATION, C.1890

BOTTOM RIGHT   A coal-fired locomotive rests at the Bathurst Train Station in the late nineteenth and early twentieth century. Passengers can be seen as they board and disembark while a horse-drawn depot hack awaits its first "taxi" fare. Water tanks situated along rail lines were a familiar sight in the days of steam-powered locomotives. The tank in the background of this photo was torn down in the early 1960s as CN converted its fleet to electric diesel. The station was erected in the late 1800s and stood until 1913 when it was destroyed by a fire. The "black robe" in the foreground is a Jesuit priest, their order being among the first Europeans to set foot on North American soil.

STEVE BRANCH ABOARD A HANDCAR (ABOVE) AND STEAM LOCOMOTIVE (BELOW)

THE CARAQUET FLYER, c. 1890

In August of 1884 work began on the Caraquet and Gulf Shore railway line and by 1890 the Caraquet Flyer was travelling up and down the coast on a daily basis hauling passengers and freight. Railway stations were constructed along the line and one was constructed in East Bathurst where the tracks crossed the Great Road to Miramichi. As this was the end of the line, a roundhouse for turning the loco-motive was also built. It was located near the East Bathurst Wharf. The Caraquet Flyer along with locomotive No. 56 is shown in the above photo at the entrance to the roundhouse with a group of railway workers and curious youngsters. The crew of the Caraquet Flyer is shown above with their locomotive. From left to right: Charlie Boudreau, Tom Glazier, Frank Couture, Henry L. Doucet, Stewart Hinton, Jack Kane, Dolph Blanchard, John Rennie (Machinist), Mark Lannigan, Henry Lavigne (sitting on pilot), Joe Lannigan, (sitting on pilot), Milton Doherty (engineer), Henry Doucet (fireman) and Norrie Boucher.

THE CARAQUET FLYER WITH O.T. CARTER, ENGINEER AND HIS CREW, AUGUST, 1884

In 1904 the New Brunswick Legislature empowered the Twin Tree Mines Railway Company to build a railway line from their mine site near Austin Brook to Gloucester Junction. Construction of the line began in 1910 to give rail access to an iron mine at Grand Falls on the Nepisiguit River. The new railway was known as The Northern New Brunswick and Seaboard Railway and in spite of its long and imposing title it was reputed to be the shortest standard gauge railway in the world. When the rail line first opened a steam powered locomotive ran on the sixteen-mile run until the mine at Grand Falls closed in 1913. As there was then no need for a steam powered train on the line the N.N.B&S railway provided passenger service with a Model T Ford car which was equipped with flanged steel wheels capable of running on the rails of the line. Stan Godin operated this primitive rail car until 1916 when the little railway ceased to operate. In 1920 the line was put back in service to transport men and materials to Grand Falls during construction of a hydro-electric dam there. During the years of construction a huge saddle-back steam locomotive powered the train on a twice daily schedule between Nepisiguit Junction and Grand Falls. A gasoline-powered rail car was also put into service to transport personnel to the dam site at Grand Falls. When construction was completed and the hydro-electric generating plant went into operation in 1926, steam train service was again discontinued. However, gasoline powered vehicles of one sort or another continued to travel regularly on the line until the mid-1950s and during those years the railway was operated by Lincoln LeBreton. In the early 1950s the future of the little railroad looked promising. The railroad was operating at a profit hauling construction materials and men to the newly opened Brunswick Mine site. In 1955 prosperity was turned to ruin. A fire destroyed the railway's only rail car and a few months later a new highway was pushed through the wilderness to the mine site. Two years later the rails of the Northern New Brunswick and Seaboard Railway was torn up and sold as scrap metal.

STEEL WHEELS TOUR

During the years that the Northern New Brunswick and Seaboard Railway ran, their were a number of jitneys and trollies that plied its rails. To transport dignitaries and guests of the Bathurst Company to their lodge on the Nepisiguit River, a bright red 1949 Ford van was outfitted with special wheels to ride the rails.

OPEN MODEL TROLLEY ON THE N.N.B&S, MID-1920S

TOP RIGHT

This open model trolley was a general purpose vehicle and it was used to haul passengers and supplies on the N.N.B&S, as well as to patrol the line. The gentleman leaning on the trundle holding his pipe is Gilbert "Lincoln" LeBreton. LeBreton piloted the famous jitneys on two round trips a day between Nepisiguit Junction and Bathurst Mines. He also was general superintendent, dispatcher, passenger agent, conductor, engineer, brakeman, baggage handler, yard foreman, mechanic and section hand. Mr. LeBreton ran the railway from the 1920s to the mid-1950s. In this period his passengers ranged from a governor general of Canada to a live moose. All manner of supplies and baggage also travelled by rail in his trolley as it was the only means of transportation to and from Bathurst Mines in those years. This photo was taken in the mid-1920s.

PRIMITIVE RAIL CAR ON THE N.N.B&S

BOTTOM RIGHT

When the Northern New Brunswick and Seaboard Railway first opened the way to Grand Falls, service was provided with a Model-T Ford, specially equipped with steel-plated wheels. Stan Godin operated the primitive rail car until 1916 and our photo shows a group of men posing with the contraption at Nepisiguit Junction.

OPEN MODEL TROLLEY (ABOVE) AND PRIMITIVE RAIL CAR (BELOW) ON THE N.N.B&S

Old Cars of Bathurst

The exact date that the first horseless carriage made its appearance in Bathurst is debatable but among the first automobiles to drive the streets of the town were those of Dr. McNichol; Peter Leger; Theatre owner, Dr. C.J. Veniot; Thomas D. Adams, New York businessman and lumber baron, and a company vehicle owned by the Bathurst Lumber Company. The Bathurst Lumber Company purchased a Franklin Air cooled vehicle in 1906 to chauffeur the company executives around town.

George Schrier, who was hired to operate the vehicle was quite unfamiliar with the new contraption and drove it in first gear for a week until he finally discovered that the car had a gearbox. Upon discovering the higher gear ratios and faster speeds the chauffeur upset the vehicle while descending the Village Hill.

Around the same year that the Bathurst Company acquired their new vehicle, Dr. McNichol purchased a gas-driven automobile to use when he made house calls.

Twenty-two year-old Arthur Smith was the driver and on one occasion he even ventured as far as Miscou Island, a distance of over fifty miles to take the doctor on a duck hunting excursion. Back at the turn-of-the-century when a gas-powered vehicle drove through the streets of Bathurst it caused a great sensation among the people.

On one such occasion when Dr. McNichol's vehicle passed Stacey's shingle mill all the hired hands at the mill rushed to the window for a look. As fate would have it, this mill had an unusual furnace for burning chips and sawdust. It was located under a steel floor in part of the mill and on this particular day, a steel cover over the furnace was left open. As the workers rushed to see the passing car one of the men ran headlong into the opening, falling to the flames below and his death.

There have been several attempts over the years at identifying the first automobile to appear on the streets of Bathurst. Although no one can be certain who owned Bathurst's first gas-powered vehicle, the ones pictured on the next page must most certainly be among the earliest, if not the very first ones.

The above vehicle was owned by Thomas A. Adams, a New York businessman who was a major shareholder of the Adams Burns Company, forerunner of the Bathurst pulp mill. Mr. Adams spent the summers in Bathurst from 1890 until his death in 1914. We can estimate the year of the vehicle to be around 1903, as the lack of front doors and the old gas lights make it appear quite ancient and it is known that Mr. Adams gave the automobile to a boy called Albert Melanson in 1911 when it stopped working. The young lad, who was a gifted mechanic, had the car running again in short order and used it regularly until he went overseas. He joined the Canadian Overseas Expeditionary Forces, 165 Battalion and went overseas in 1916. He became a pilot and died in an airplane crash in 1918.

THE LANDRY CLAN IN THEIR MODEL-T, 1938

A Sunday excursion to Youghall Beach was a summer tradition for the Landry family. This photograph taken in 1938 in front of their Queen Street home shows the entire Landry clan, with Gilbert Landry at the controls, aboard their Model-T Ford and ready for a trip to the beach.

THE BATHURST FLUSHER, C. 1920

This unusual vehicle is an International Chassis truck with water tank and flushing pipes attached. It was called a "Flusher" and older residents remember these types of vehicles (some horse drawn) being used to keep the dust down on the town's streets before they were paved in 1932. This circa 1920 photograph is believed to have been taken somewhere in Quebec where the Chassis was sent to be outfitted for commercial use as a street flusher and water tanker.

DR. MCNICHOL'S CAR, AND CHAUFFEUR, 1912

This vehicle was photographed in 1912. It was owned by one of Bathurst's earliest and most prominent physicians, Dr. McNichol. The vehicle was chauffeured by a young Janeville man, twenty-two-year-old Arthur Smith, shown with the car. We could not determine the make of the vehicle but the right-hand drive steering wheel reveals it as a Canadian or European make as Canadian drivers only switched to left-hand drive in 1922.

HOMEMADE SOFT DRINKS FOR SALE

Around 1919, Messrs. Bosca and Buraglia purchased machinery to manufacture soft drinks and set up shop in East Bathurst, where they had already established a successful grocery story and bakery business. They brewed Ginger Ale, Iron Brew and Gazóse, a famous Italian recipe, from the country from which they emigrated in 1908. That same year they also bought a new 1919 Ford from Albert Hinton to deliver their products. The above photo shows the motor truck, loaded with cases of soft drinks. Posing with their brand new vehicle are, L-R: Waldo Bosca, Thomas Buraglia, Mario Bosca, and Claude Buraglia. Incidentally, the earliest known bottler of soft drinks in Bathurst was John Ellis. He operated a barber shop and bottling works on Water Street around 1890.

THE HAPPY GANG OUT FOR A SUNDAY DRIVE

TOP RIGHT

The photograph at top right was taken around 1941 and the automobile shown is a 1917 Willys-Overland, four-door soft top touring sedan. As for the "passengers," they were known as the "Happy Gang." Shown seated in the car from left are Harvey Babin, Paula Doucet, Wilbur Elhatton, Mary Elhatton, and Edgar Alain. Standing: Cletus Elhatton, Earl Doucet, Rupert Doucet, Jerry Elhatton, Maurita Elhatton, Joan Power, James Babin, Vaughn Elhatton, and Edward Sears. The location is near the former Kent's store on Main Street. There have been many changes since this photograph was taken fifty-five years ago (the first, of course, being that Kent's store no longer exists). The carefree way of filling the old jalopy to standing-room capacity for a Sunday drive would not be acceptable under today's laws; the car does not look like it would pass registered safety inspection. However, although four people strapped into one of today's air-conditioned sedans would be safer and more comfortable, we cannot help but think that the above arrangement looks to be a lot more fun.

MORE SUNDAY DRIVERS, c. 1925

BOTTOM RIGHT

The bottom right photograph pictures a more sedate group of people taking a ride in what appears to be a vehicle of about 1925 vintage. The automobile industry was still in its infancy in the 1920s and a ride in the family sedan was a pleasurable event, especially for youngsters.

THE HAPPY GANG (ABOVE) AND MORE SUNDAY DRIVERS, C. 1925 (BELOW)

**LEGER'S
BAKERY
TRUCK,
1920**

Back in 1919, J.P. Leger and son established a bakery on Water Street in Bathurst. It was located in the basement of the Old Opera House. The bakery was very modern for its time, with up-to-date machinery which included a bread mixer, molder and divider, bread wrapper, and a cake machine operated by four individual drive electric motors. A Middleby oven could turn out 2,500 loaves in ten hours. The best Manitoba hard wheat was used in each loaf. A junior member of the firm, H.J. Leger, conveyed the bakery goods to all parts of town in a motor delivery truck. This photo, taken in 1920, shows the delivery vehicle with H.J. Leger at the wheel.

**MAPLE
LEAF
BAKERS**

The Maple Leaf Bread Company also delivered bread and pastries in the Bathurst area in the 1920s and 1930s. The delivery vehicle is shown parked on Water Street in front of The McKenna Brothers Building. The Moncton based company opened a branch in Bathurst in 1927 in the Old Opera House building on Main Street.

PETER LEGER'S 1910 BUICK RUNABOUT

Leading Bathurst businessman and early automobile enthusiast, Peter J. Leger sits at the wheel of his 1910 Buick Runabout. He is accompanied by his girlfriend, Miss Evelyn Rennie. Mr. Leger operated the town's first motion picture theatre.

DR. J.C. VENIOT, IN HIS 1912 BUICK

Doctor J.C. Veniot, along with his wife and infant daughter, sits in his 1912 McLaughlan Buick open sedan. Mr. Veniot served as MP for Gloucester and was Mayor of Bathurst at one time. He was also appointed to the senate.

SUMMER SUNDAYS AND MODEL T'S The motor vehicle was becoming a popular means of transportation and many excursions were taken to the countryside on summer Sundays. The women pictured above are enjoying just such an outing in their model-T Ford of that era.

A SPRING OUTING TO THE FALLS A Sunday outing to Tetagouche Falls was a popular and common occurrence in the early part of the century. This group had their photo taken at the falls on May 26th, 1913. It must have been a cool day that May as the ladies are all dressed in heavy coats and the men have their overcoats buttoned to the top. Horse-drawn carriages were the means of transportation back then, and three excellent examples of such a vehicle can be seen along with a pair of fine horses.

Ships

The Bathurst Harbour was a busy place in the early years of this century, with ships delivering and taking on cargo on a regular basis. Tugboats were also a common sight in the harbour in those years. The *St. Anne, Nepisiguit*, the *Betty D*, the *Peggy L.,* and the *Frances Huntley* among other lesser known vessels; the *Albert L, Gordon C.,* and the oldest one of memory, the *Nyanza,* have all sailed into history.

Bathurst was also a natural location for shipbuilding because of its sheltered harbours and abundance of timber. Among the many shipyards that operated in Bathurst, the most famous one carried the Cunard name. Others that followed were Smith's, Wolhaupter, Woolner, Ferguson, Rankin and Co., Meahan, Millar, Gammon, Daly, O'Brien, Gibbs, and Mullaly. Hundreds of wooden sailing vessels were launched from Bathurst's shipyards; some destined to work in the harbour while others sailed around the world.

When the age of steel ships and steam engines arrived, Bathurst craftsmen turned to the task of constructing this new type of vessel and their handiwork could be seen on the waters of the bay as they replaced the wooden sailing ships.

THE NEPISIGUIT IN BATHURST HARBOUR.

The *St. Anne*, a steel rescue tug officially numbered 143283, was built by Ferguson Bros. at Port Glasgow, Scotland and arrived in Bathurst in July of 1924. She measured 135 feet by twenty-nine feet, with a depth of sixteen feet. She weighted 465 tons and was powered by a 1,200 horse power coal-fired steam engine.

The ship, later renamed the *Cascapedia* during the war years, was loaned to the navy during the winter months, when she was not used by Bathurst Power and Paper. She saw service in the Second World War as a minesweeper, and after the war, returned to being a tug boat.

THE
BETTY D,
c. 1920

The *Betty D.* was a Bathurst Company tugboat that plied her trade in Bathurst Harbour in the 1920s. She is shown sitting in the Bathurst Harbour with the company's East Bathurst mill in the background.

SCHOONER LOADING LUMBER, BOUND FOR NEW YORK

The three-masted schooner tied up at Billy White's Wharf in Bathurst is the *Daniel Getson*. She was loading laths and long lumber processed at White's mill. In the early 1930s, when this photograph was taken, many shipments of the type were consigned from Bathurst to Manhattan, New York. The *Daniel Geston* was built in Bridgewater, N.S. by N.A. Naugler for the man whose name she bore and who hailed from LaHave, Nova Scotia. In the mid-1930s, she was sold to G.O. Henricksen of Weymouth, Nova Scotia and her captain, Arthur Moore died on board in 1935. Then, in 1938, the graceful craft was sold to Howard L. Sutton, of Silver Lake, N.Y. and renamed *Wanderthirst*. There is no record after that, except that she was still in existence in the 1940s.

CARGO SHIPS BOUND FOR EUROPE

Not infrequent sights in Bathurst Harbour in the mid-1930s were cargo ships like this one tied up at the Gloucester Lumber and Trading Co. Ltd. wharf off lower Main Street. This particular vessel, of foreign registry, was being loaded with a shipment of lumber consigned to the European market, including Germany.

**THE
ANNIE R
PASSENGER
BOAT,
1909**

This photo of a steam-powered passenger boat, which used to run between
Bathurst and Carron Point and Youghall Beach, was taken in 1909. The craft was
called the *Annie R.* She was manned by a crew of three: Captain Jack Stever, Purser
Percy Rennie and Engineer Norey Boucher. Thirty-six feet long and eight-feet wide,
the *Annie* R., equipped with a steam boiler and engine, was built by Joe Stackhouse
of West Saint John when he was engaged on construction of the Nepisiguit Lumber
Co. mill in East Bathurst. The boat took form in the second storey of the George
Eddy Co. Ltd. plant and was the property of John Rennie, foreman of the then
Caraquet and Gulf Shore Railway. She had a complement of twenty-five passengers, and the return fare to the Points from town was a quarter. Automobiles were
few in those days and you went to the beach by either boat, livery horse or on foot.
Standing on the bow, to the extreme right, is Captain Jack, who also held the
distinction of being Bathurst's first taxicab operator.

Fires and Blazes

RESIDENTS DRAWN TO THE FLAMES—GREAT FIRE OF 1914

Household furnishings and mercantile goods of all manner are
piled in the streets and Bathurst residents turn out to watch the
great fire of 1914 as flames threaten the Sweeney Hotel.

When we recall the many devastating fires that have struck Bathurst over the years, some of those that first come to mind are the Dunn Hospital, the Gloucester Hospital, and, of course, the great fire of 1914. But one such tragedy that is all but forgotten is the fire of July 20, 1874. The blaze originated from a spark igniting the roof of a building near the store of Sutherland and Desbois. The *Union Advocate* newspaper reported the event with a frankness that certainly did not present a very good image of Bathurst's fire department:

> A heavy wind prevailed at the time and this, combined with extraordinary stupidity and want of organization on the part of the firewardens, has resulted in twenty-seven buildings being consumed. The fire spread with great rapidity, the only appliance for subduing the flames being a Burn's small-hand engine and buckets. Ferguson's engine arrived some time after the fire commenced but could not be managed—the Boss & DesBresey store, containing a large quantity of tinware and stores; the residences of Mells, Boss, Albert Carter, Armstrong, Proctor, Malloy; a number of small shops, and the railway offices. The loss totalled $25,000, with Carter's hotel alone valued at $1,200.

On April 29 of 1914 disaster struck again. A spark flying from a kitchen stove in the Holdengraber residence and igniting a pot of tar caused one of the most disastrous fires in Bathurst history. A complete city block was destroyed by the conflagration. Thirty-five buildings were destroyed, among them Lounsburys store, the telephone exchange, the Masonic Hall, the fire station, private residences, warehouses, and barns.

The fire raged for a full day fanned by a light breeze that carried sparks and burning embers to nearby buildings. The citizens of the town fought the fires with wet blankets and bucket brigades until the intense heat drove them away from the buildings. Merchandise of all types and the contents of many homes and businesses was piled on the streets only to be consumed by the flames as the fire spread.

When the Sweeney Hotel was doomed to destruction a gang of toughs broke into the bar and carried away its stock of liquors.

Likewise, some of the unprotected goods that was taken from various stores and piled in the streets was carried away by the armload by thieves. A number of special constables were sworn in to protect private property and keep order in the town. At the time the fire broke out the town's fire engine was out testing the strength of a new horse that had just been put into duty.

The engine was near the old post office when the alarm rang. The horse was not able to move fast enough with the heavy engine so another one was pressed into service and the engine was hurried to Reads Wharf where it was placed in position to take on water. The brave firemen with the help of private citizens fought the blaze until mid-afternoon when the towns of Newcastle and Campbellton were called for help from the burning telephone exchange and a special train was sent out from each town with men, equipment and supplies.

By nightfall, the flames were brought under control and water was continued to be poured on the smoldering ruins throughout the night. In the morning of April 30 the citizens awoke to face the horrific destruction that the fire had wrought and began plans to rebuild.

On November 26 of 1924, a devastating fire broke out in East Bathurst consuming almost the entire business district. The fire started in Boulay's Pool Hall. As the town had no fire protection or water supply, the fire raged uncontrolled consuming seven buildings. An old fire engine that had been stored for many years was put into service and a quarter mile of hose was stretched from a water supply, but was of very little use in quenching the inferno. The engine only delivered a few buckets of water before it ceased to operate.

THE GREAT FIRE OF 1914   The charred remains of homes and businesses are all that remain after the great fire of 1914. The Robertson Hotel and barns as well as the wooden sidewalks escaped the blaze.

BATHURST FIRE DEPARTMENT, 1938

It was in 1916, five years after incorporation, that the Town of Bathurst formed its first organized fire department, entirely of volunteers. It was aptly called the Keystone Fire Brigade and operated under the direction of Chief Robert C. (Bob) Rogers. The brigade's modest equipment in those early years was drawn by a sturdy and spirited team of horses. The situation continued thus until 1929, when a Model A Ford chassis was acquired as the basis of a fire truck. In addition to the fire truck, the brigade had the following equipment at its disposal: extension wooden ladder, twenty-gallon soda and acid extinguisher, several axes, six hundred feet of two-and-a-half inch hose, and lanterns for lighting purposes. In the above photograph taken in 1938 at the Bathurst fire station, Fire Chief Frank Brennan sits at the controls of the 1928 Model T Ford.